IMAGES
of America

WOODLAND PARK

This photograph is of Woodland Park in 2009 as seen from the Woodland Park Library. Pikes Peak dominates the southern skyline of Woodland Park and has been a beacon to Colorado pioneers since the 1859 gold rush days, "Pikes Peak or Bust." The hardy souls who made this journey are the source of the cultural heritage of this region. (Ute Pass Historical Society; photograph by Gary Demig.)

ON THE COVER: The Free Methodist Church stands on the southwest corner of Park and Henrietta Streets in 1886. This photograph is thought to have been taken by Ira Rudy of Cascade. Both women and men are shown carrying a casket in what is clearly a funeral procession, although the decorations on the hearse do not seem to fit the occasion. (Ute Pass Historical Society, Carroll.)

IMAGES
of America

WOODLAND PARK

Ute Pass Historical Society
and Pikes Peak Museum

ARCADIA
PUBLISHING

Copyright © 2010 by Ute Pass Historical Society and Pikes Peak Museum
ISBN 978-1-5316-5330-9

Published by Arcadia Publishing
Charleston, South Carolina

Library of Congress Control Number: 2009941027

For all general information contact Arcadia Publishing at:
Telephone 843-853-2070
Fax 843-853-0044
E-mail sales@arcadiapublishing.com
For customer service and orders:
Toll-Free 1-888-313-2665

Visit us on the Internet at www.arcadiapublishing.com

*This book is dedicated to the Ute Pass Historical Society's
founders and the devoted patrons and volunteers who
have kept the society going through the years.*

CONTENTS

ACKNOWLEDGMENTS

The Ute Pass Historical Society (UPHS) thanks the local residents who shared their knowledge of the history of our area from the 1920s through the 1990s, including Chet Koons, Ric Hermann, Dan and Anita Starr, H. Madeline Spielman Gappa, Elene Spielman Kile, Naomi Markus, Ellen Carlson, and Donna Clifford. We also thank the Ute Pass Social Club, Dot Blanton, and Jan Petit for researching, writing, and collaborating on a proposed book celebrating the centennial of Woodland Park that served as an important resource for this book. Finally, thank you to the Ute Pass Historical Society volunteers who collaborated on this book, including Larry Black, Gary Demig, Donna Finicle, Marcia Ford, Paul Loyd, George Parkhurst, Vern Renter, Harold Shippey, Jean Taylor, Mary Ann Davis, and Jane Lass.

INTRODUCTION

Woodland Park, Colorado, is called "The City Above The Clouds" for good reason. Nestled among pines, spruce, and aspens at an altitude of 8,465 feet, Woodland Park often enjoys blue skies and brilliant sunshine even as gray clouds settle over its lower-altitude neighbors. Today it's a city of about 8,000 year-round residents, but for several hundred years, the area was home to the Ute Indians, who were, not surprisingly, known as the Blue Sky People.

In the mid-1800s, American prospectors and settlers began to travel from Colorado City, now part of modern-day Colorado Springs, 18 miles to the east of modern Woodland Park, along a trail now known as the Ute Pass Indian Trail. The pass took them more than 3,000 feet higher into the Rocky Mountains, along Fountain Creek on the North Slope of Pikes Peak. By the late 1880s, the Colorado Midland Railway was bringing even more people up the pass—and to a spot known as both Summit Park and Manitou Park. With its incorporation in 1891, the whistle stop became the town of Woodland Park. At the time, the town boasted 122 residents, a hardware store, a blacksmith shop, a drugstore, a furniture store, and a saddle and livery business.

The early days were dominated by the timber industry, with the area providing lumber first for railway construction and later for the gold mines that sprang up in nearby Cripple Creek and Victor. At the time, visitors to the area could see piles of lumber and railroad ties stretching along the entire length of Woodland Park's main street. In the 1890s, the gold rush in Cripple Creek and Victor contributed to the lively commerce in the town, with people and gold passing through Woodland Park as they made their way up and down the pass.

Early on, tourists began to discover the natural beauty of the area, while tuberculosis patients were discovering the healing properties of the clean mountain air, prompting one publication to describe the city as a "charming health resort." In 1872, Dr. William Bell, founder of the town of Manitou Springs to the east, purchased land north of town to create a true resort hotel, which he called the Manitou Park Hotel. This country club–type facility featured 35 rooms, a golf course, lawn tennis, music, and dancing. A horse-drawn carriage known as a "tally-ho" made two trips a day between Manitou Park and the future Woodland Park. In addition to operating the resort, Dr. Bell also harvested timber. He built a short railroad line, nicknamed the "No Name Railroad," to transport the wood to mills north of Woodland Park.

In 1889, Mrs. James Green opened the first hotel in Woodland Park. She named the 15-room hotel The Crest. It stood on the northeast corner of Park and Lake Avenues until 1910, when the hotel was dismantled and its lumber recycled. With the arrival of more tourists came the need for more hotel rooms. In 1892, the 42-room Woodland Hotel was built, with a distinctive "witch's hat" roof over the front cupola. During the 1920s, the hotel, located on Lorraine Avenue, served as a tuberculosis sanitarium before being torn down in 1939. Oral histories from the time indicate that even after the sanitarium closed, local children put the building to good use. They would roller-skate on the front porch and slide down the laundry chute to the basement.

The first school in the area was the Spielman School in Manitou Park, near the site of the Paint Pony Ranch. In 1890, a number of small schools in the Ute Pass area became consolidated into the two-teacher Woodland School. The two-story frame building housed the lower grades on the first floor and the upper grades on the second floor. In later years, when the town was without a church building, the school was also used for church services. Still later, a church was used for kindergarten classes. In 1924, further consolidation brought students from nearby Crystola, Manitou Park, and an area to the west known as Edlowe. That called for the hiring of a third teacher.

Starting in 1926, older students made the commute to Manitou Springs for high school. Eventually, a junior-senior high school was built in Woodland Park, and over the years, various buildings in town were used to house different grade levels. Today, the Woodland Park School District includes three elementary schools, a middle school, and a high school, with a total enrollment of about 3,200 students. Students come from Woodland Park, Divide, and Florissant, as well as other areas if space is available.

About 3 miles west of town was the Skelton Ranch, one of the first dude ranches in the Woodland Park area. Owned by Judge W. T. Skelton, the 2,000-acre ranch was located atop a high ridge that offered panoramic views of the area. The ranch, which featured locally raised chickens and locally grown food, was accessible by stagecoach. It was later used by Boy Scouts and other groups. Eventually the land was donated to the million-acre Pike National Forest, which provides a natural boundary for Woodland Park and limits the city's geographic expansion.

Paradise Ranch, a 400-acre ranch operated by Frank Snell that dates back to 1928, was located just to the east of Woodland Park on U.S. Highway 24. It was one of the last dude ranches in the Woodland Park area. Two signs of its existence remain; a tunnel under the highway that connected the lodge site to the former rodeo grounds area, now a shopping center, and the lodge building itself. This ranch was popular with Easterners who came by rail to ride horses in the Wild West.

Operating alongside the dude ranches were the many working ranches in and around the Woodland Park area. Many of the working ranches were started on 160-acre tracts granted under the Homestead Act of 1862. A few of the original ranches still survive.

In the pages that follow, the reader will discover almost 200 photographs of this historically fascinating area. The Ute Pass Historical Society is pleased to share these photographs, along with brief introductions to the people, places, and industries that have given Woodland Park its distinctive character.

One

THE BLUE SKY PEOPLE

The first people to live in present-day Woodland Park were the Ute Indians. Ute is the word from which Utah is derived. To American settlers, the Utes became known as the Blue Sky People, living high above the clouds in what they called the "shining mountains," the Rocky Mountains of Colorado. At first they lived in bark-covered huts called wickiups and later in teepees made from elk or buffalo hides. Archaeologists today believe that Utes emerged as a distinct Native American people around 1300, but it was in the 1600s, when they obtained horses from the Pueblos of New Mexico, that Ute culture underwent a dramatic change. Horsemanship and horse ownership became marks of accomplishment and wealth for the Utes. From the Pueblo Indians, they also obtained cattle and sheep, which they raised and traded throughout the area.

The Utes traveled down Ute Pass to Colorado Springs and Manitou Springs, selling buffalo goods and taking the healing waters from Manitou, where they believed the Great Spirit lived. Animals, particularly the bear, served as Ute deities. Every spring after the first thunder was heard, the Utes conducted the Bear Dance ritual, but it was in the summer that the Utes held their most significant religious ritual, the Sun Dance.

Two prominent Utes were Chief Ouray and his wife, Chipeta, who traveled to Washington, D.C., several times to negotiate with government officials concerning the fate of historic Ute tribal lands. Ouray's fluency in English, Spanish, and several Native American languages, as well as his commitment to peaceful resolution of conflict, helped to create the first treaty between the Utes and the U.S. government. Several Ute reservations exist today in Utah and Southern Colorado, where about 3,500 of the 5,000 Utes live.

Pikes Peak is seen here from Woodland Park around 1900. The mountain is named for Lt. Zebulon M. Pike, who led an 1806 U.S. Army expedition to explore the southern boundaries of the Louisiana Purchase. He provided the U.S. government with the first accurate description of the area. Pike never climbed the peak that bears his name. Anna May Wellington (Armentrout) took this photograph; she was taught the techniques of photography as a teenager by her cousin Bert Smith in the late 1800s. She learned to evenly spread a wet, light-sensitive suspension on glass plates and then let the plates dry, keeping them in a light-tight enclosure. She used a timed exposure of the plate with a large view camera. Her family donated over 300 glass plate negatives of various sizes, from four-by-five inches to eight-by-ten inches, to the Ute Pass Historical Society. Anna May took photographs up and down Ute Pass, in Teller County as well as on trips to western Colorado, Colorado Springs, and Denver. (UPHS, Wellington.)

This 1935 view of Pikes Peak is from Colorado Highway 67 North between Woodland Park and Manitou Lake. In 1859, as fortune-seekers used Pikes Peak to guide them to gold discoveries near Denver and gold and silver in Leadville, they found that the Ute Pass Indian Trail, even with improvements, was inadequate. In 1871, Colorado Springs built a new road that followed Fountain Creek, at a cost of about $4000. (UPHS, Dorothy Hartman.)

Pikes Peak is seen here from Woodland Park in a Colorado Midland Railway Postcard postmarked in 1913. Pikes Peak provides a beautiful backdrop for Woodland Park. Visitors and residents enjoy the constantly changing face of the peak in storms and sunshine, from sunrise to sunset. For the local Utes, migrations around this mountain, and its changing seasons, dictated the pattern of their lives. (UPHS, Conrad Wilson.)

Buckskin Charlie was the leader of the Southern Utes at the trail ride reenactment on August 29, 1912, along the Ute Pass Indian Trail. The Ute Trail Ride started at the upper end of the trail. The trail goes east, leaving French Creek, and follows a shallow gulch to the top where it levels out. The trail continues east and starts down Rattlesnake Gulch past a present-day Colorado Springs water facility and down into Manitou Springs above Ruxton Avenue to approximately the spot where the Manitou Incline was located. The dedication was organized by the El Paso County Pioneers Association at the urging of D. N. Heizer, mayor of Colorado Springs. Heizer was also the principal owner of the Cascade Town and Improvement Company. Indian Agent Charles Adams, Buckskin Charlie, Utes from the Southern Ute Reservation near Ignacio, and other dignitaries made up the procession. Thomas Cusack of Marigreen Pines provided horses. Anne Cusack Johnson took this photograph when she was a teenager. (UPHS, Cusack.)

These Ute Indians are riding to French Creek at the 1912 Ute Indian Trail Dedication. The ancestors of these Southern Utes had contact with the Spanish in Santa Fe in the 1620s, acquiring horses from them, learning their ways, and keeping them at bay. Horses altered their lifestyle by giving them greater mobility. Hostile clashes between the Utes and settlers were rare. (UPHS, Heizer.)

Ute people from Ignacio, Colorado, are shown here after the 1912 Ute Indian Trail Dedication. Ute treaties with the Americans began in 1849, when the Tabeguache band accepted $5,000 as payment for recognizing the U.S.'s authority. In 1868, Chief Ouray succeeded in barring all whites from the western slope of Colorado. A later treaty set aside 1.5 million acres for the Confederated Ute Reservation. Later agreements changed these decisions. (UPHS, Heizer.)

13

This is another image from the Ute Indian Trail Dedication on August 29, 1912. Ute Indians from Ignacio are riding with Proctor Nichols, starting down the Ute Trail across Fountain Creek from present-day Marigreen Pines. Elinor Cottage, Thomas and Mary Cusack's family home prior to his construction of the Marigreen Pines mansion, is visible at the top left. (UPHS, Heizer.)

Ute Indians headed for French Creek from Cascade on August 29, 1912. The Dawes Act of 1887 acknowledged the right of Native Americans to become U.S. citizens and established individual Native American homesteads and tribal land. The Hunter Act of 1895 settled the southern Ute reservation land in southwestern Colorado, provided for individual, family, and tribal allotments, and include the provision that lands not claimed could be sold to whites. (UPHS, Heizer.)

This photograph was taken at the Ute encampment in Cheyenne Canyon after the Ute Pass Trail Dedication ride on August 29, 1912. Eagle Eye is shown along with several other Utes in the background. He is performing a pipe ceremony, a sacred ritual for connecting physical and spiritual worlds. The pipe enables prayer in a physical form, with the smoke as the words, which go out and touch everything. It becomes a part of all that is. Smoke coming from the pipe symbolizes the truth being spoken and the smoke provides a path for prayers to reach the Great Spirit, and for the Great Spirit to travel down to the earth. Pipe ceremonies were widely used among native peoples in this country. Eagle Eye is using a pipe typical of the Plains Indians, with a wooden stem, a pipestone bowl, and decorative feathers. (UPHS, Stumbough.)

These Ute Indians camped in Cheyenne Canyon in 1912. In the back row (fourth from the right) is Buckskin Charlie, sporting a peace medal. He succeeded Ouray as the leader of the Utes. Seated, third from the right, is Ouray's wife, Chipeta. Sixth from the right is the spiritual leader Nanace, seated with a blanket on his shoulder and a headdress in his lap. (UPHS, Virginia Stumbough.)

Ute Indians dance with a white woman and child at the Ute Indian Trail Dedication in 1912. The white woman and child are thought to be Mary Green Cusack, Thomas Cusack's second wife, and their son, David. The Cusacks built their new home, Marigreen Pines, about 10 years after this photograph was taken, in memory of Mary, who died in 1922. (UPHS, David Cusack.)

Indian agent Charles Adams (left), Colorado Springs mayor and president of the Cascade Town Company David N. Heizer (center), and Buckskin Charlie are shown placing the first Ute Pass Trail Marker (UPT) in front of the Gardener house in Cascade on August 29, 1912. The marker is at center-right, in the grass just below front car wheel. He had been a close friend of Ouray and had been on several of the treaty trips to Washington, D.C., with the Ute Indian delegations. His Ute name was Sepiah. He was of the Capote Band of the southern Utes and, like Ouray, was part Apache. In the same sense that Ouray was leader of all the Utes, Buckskin Charlie cooperated with the government agencies while keeping faith with the traditional Ute customs and ceremonies, even when in conflict with the government agencies. Buckskin Charlie died in 1936 at the age of 96. (UPHS, Heizer.)

Here is the procession for the Ute Indian Trail Ride in 1912. The original Ute trail went from French Creek in Cascade (10 miles east of Woodland Park) along the ridge on the south side of the drainage. It goes east and levels out at the top, then starts down Rattlesnake Gulch into Manitou Springs above Ruxton Avenue. (UPHS; photograph by Ann Cusack Johnson.)

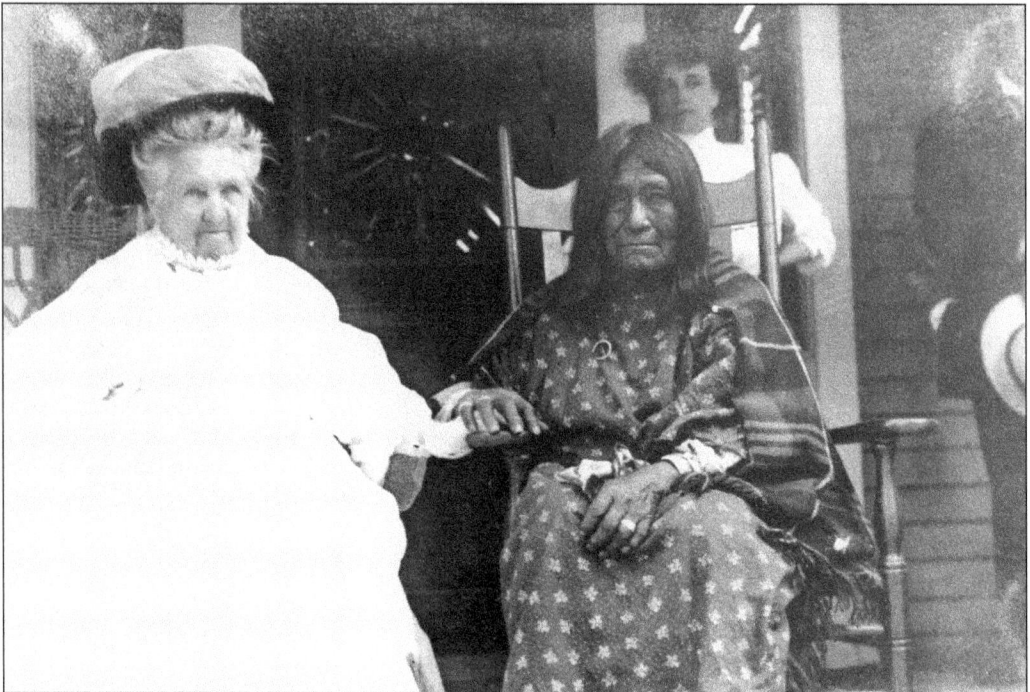

Chipeta visits with Mrs. Charles Adams (left) in 1912. Chipeta, wife of the famous Ute leader Ouray, had ridden 150 miles on a pony and 300 miles on the railroad to visit Mrs. Adams and help mark the Ute Pass Indian Trail. At the urging of Colorado Springs mayor David N. Heizer, the event was organized by the El Paso County Pioneers Association. (Colorado Springs Pioneers Museum.)

The 'Old Boy' Himself.

The photographer, Anna May Wellington, titled this photograph "The Old Boy Himself." It is thought to refer to Colorow (right of center), a Ute Indian leader who was a member of a small group of northern Utes that came to be called the White River Band. He was thought to be part of the leadership involved in the killing of Indian Agent Nathan Meeker, along with several other white Indian agency employees. Meeker reportedly had ordered the plowing up a Ute source of amusement, a horse racetrack, in order to plant potatoes. Other events culminated in Colorado governor Frederick Pitkin's proclamation that "The Utes must go," which resulted in the removal of Ute bands from most of Colorado in 1880. Colorow paid little attention to the fact that Utes were being moved to reservations in Colorado and Utah. Despite many attempts to capture him—two even involving his meeting with the governor of Colorado—he continued to roam freely throughout Colorado until his death. (UPHS, Wellington.)

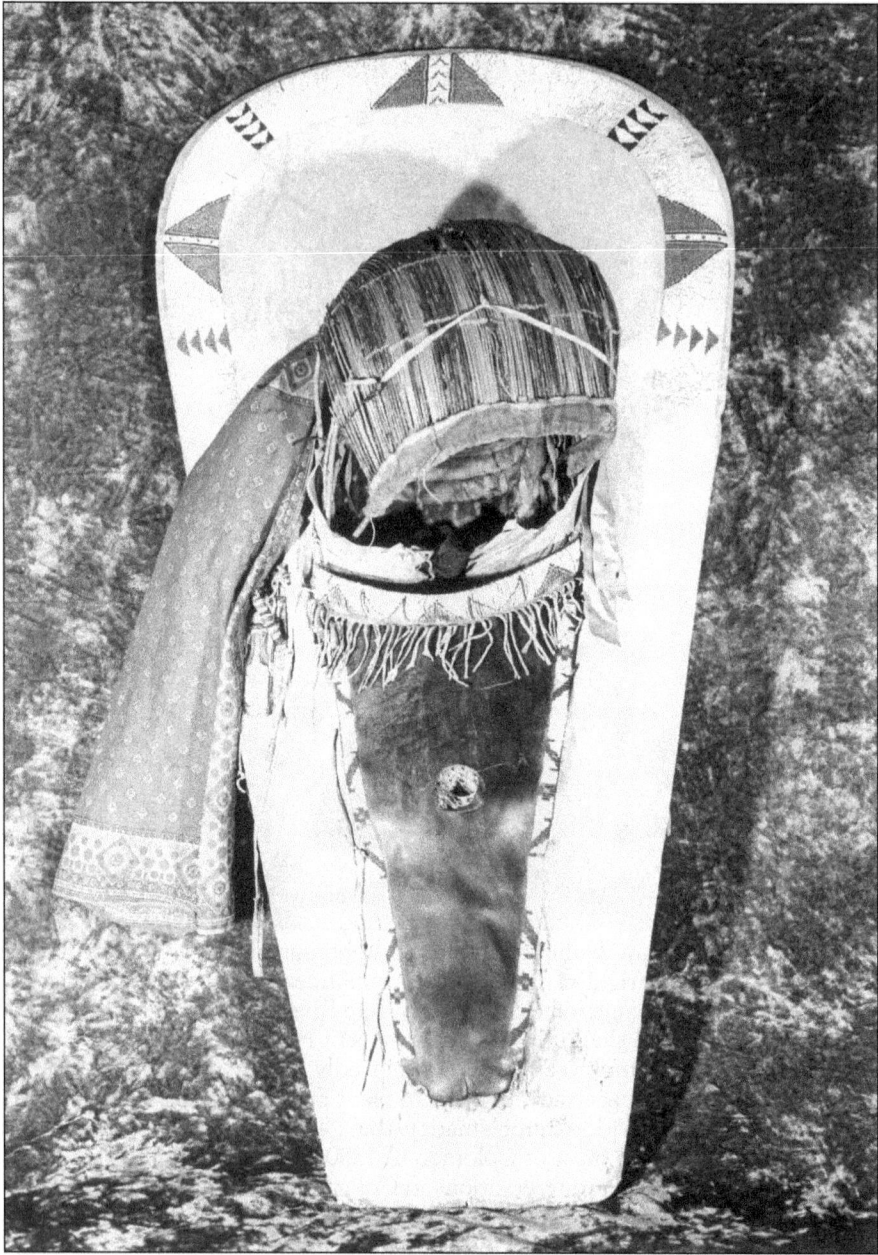

The Ute Pass Historical Society purchased this c.1885 Ute Indian cradleboard for $4,250 in 1989. It had been on loan to the U.S. National Museum, Smithsonian Institution, from 1918 to 1938. It was then returned to the owner and subsequently sold several times to private collectors. It is 45 inches in height and 22 inches wide at the top, covered in white deerskin and beaded on the upper edge. The beadwork is exceptional. The willow hood is in almost perfect condition. The cradleboard was tied on the back for a large baby and shows sweat stains from use. Attached is the medicine bundle containing the umbilical cord and other significant items such as a bow of twined twigs, a tepee carved on an elk bugler, a tiny perfume bottle from San Francisco, and a long green beaded strip and charms of elk tooth and horn to amuse the child. Johnathan Batkin of the Taylor Museum said, "It is the finest that I have seen." (UPHS.)

John M. Huiskamp was a Dutch artist, hunter, and adventurer. He left Keokuk, Iowa, early in 1850 headed for the California gold fields. Ute Indians in Manitou Springs befriended him and he took a trip with them up the Ute Trail to a high pass overlooking South Park. He reportedly spent three years traveling with the Utes throughout south-central Colorado. When he returned to Iowa, he rolled up his beaded Native American saddlebags around his tobacco pouch, knife sheath, knife, and buffalo horn spoon and packed them away. He is shown here after his return to Iowa in a long, fur-trimmed coat and hat (Wales Art Studio, Keokuk, Iowa). The Huiskamp artifacts were passed down through the family and are believed to be some of the oldest known examples of Ute cultural material ever collected. (UPHS, Huiskamp Collection, John Alexander.)

John M. Huiskamp collected these items in the 1850s. His descendant, John Huiskamp Alexander, believed these artifacts should be returned to the region where they were collected. He lent the items to UPHS in 1976, and in 1979, his widow donated them in memory of her husband. The beadwork and condition of the items are remarkable. (UPHS, Huiskamp Collection, Mrs. John Alexander.)

This Native American powwow photograph is from an event held in Woodland Park in August of 1994. The Lone Tree Council (and later the Lone Feather Council) organized powwows for about 10 years. The two- and three-day powwows eventually moved to Calhan, Colorado Springs, and other venues. A small Saturday afternoon event in Memorial Park was resurrected in August of 2009. (UPHS, Doris Breitenfeld.)

Two

A NEW NAME FOR
A NEW TOWN

Between 1888 and 1890, some citizens of the Ute Pass area formed the Woodland Park Town Company. They filed a claim for water rights with state engineers on September 29, 1890. Apparently, they had already decided they wanted the town to be named Woodland Park instead of Manitou Park. On December 1st of that year, they met at Baldwin's store and voted to incorporate the town of Woodland Park, which at the time consisted of 122 residents. Notice of the vote was posted ahead of time at eight locations, including stores, private homes, a restaurant, a telegraph pole, and prominent trees. Some 38 votes were cast, 24 in favor and 14 against, and the town of Woodland Park was born. The official incorporation date was January 26, 1891.

The young town became known as a resort area with a potential for business investment. An unidentified journalist described the new town as follows: "Nature designed this spot as a resting place for the weary and our overworked humanity as well as for those who have a love for the grand and beautiful and the means to enjoy them. The only thing lacking was the wealth and energy of man to smooth down the rough places and supply those accessories to pleasure and comfort which nature cannot provide."

Another article touted Woodland Park as a distribution center for the mining camps, a promising mining camp in its own right, a halfway station between Colorado Springs and Cripple Creek, and the stage terminal for Manitou Park and the West Creek mining camps. All of which "serve[d] to make of it the leading city between Colorado Springs, Cripple Creek, and Leadville, both from a commercial as well as a mining standpoint."

All of that makes early Woodland Park sound like a respectable town. Even so, it had its share of problems. The town saw fit to pass a "morals and decency" ordinance within three months of its incorporation. They soon built a small calaboose (jail) to help enforce these first laws. The new town grew as the residents created businesses, homes, schools and churches, and the Colorado Midland Railway—built in 1887—connected it all to points east and west.

This image shows Woodland Park looking west in about 1900. Pikes Peak is out of the picture on the left, south of town. The photograph shows the main street, Midland Avenue (now U.S. Highway 24), with a Colorado Midland Railway boxcar on the railroad tracks to the left, the Woodland Hotel in the background to the left, and the Battey Brothers Grocery. (UPHS, Wellington.)

Here is Woodland Park around 1935, looking from the west end of Midland Avenue. The vacant Midland Eating House was purchased by A. D. Hackman and moved across the street to the north side of Midland Avenue. The Mansard roof was raised and changed to a hip roof for more second-story room, and the building received a new name—Midland Hotel. (Hartman.)

This photograph is a copy of the official May 16, 1902, notification of acceptance from the U.S. Post Office Department of A. D. Hackman's proposal for a mail route between South Platte and Woodland Park. Previous unofficial post offices in the area had been at the Junction House, Terrill's store, Summit Park, and Manitou Park. (UPHS.)

One of the first stores in Woodland Park, N. W. Terrill's dry goods store is shown here in 1890. It thrived during the peak of the Cripple Creek gold boom and remained a dry goods store through the 1960s. In 1967, it became the Cowhand, a western wear store, which in 2009 is owned and operated by Merry Jo Larsen. (UPHS; photograph by Jan Petit.)

ACCEPTANCE.

Post Office Department,

OFFICE OF THE SECOND ASSISTANT POSTMASTER GENERAL,

Washington, D. C., May 16, 1902.

Sir:

The POSTMASTER GENERAL has accepted your proposal, under advertisement of January 18, 1902, for conveying the United States Mail on Colorado Route No. 65183 between South Platte and Woodland Park

" WITH CELERITY, CERTAINTY, AND SECURITY,"

from July 1, 1902, to June 30, 1906, at $ 240.00 a year.

Contracts will be sent in due time to the Postmaster at your place of residence, which you must execute, and file in the Department within 30 days from this date; otherwise you will be declared a failing bidder, and the service will be re-let at your expense.

The notice to accepted bidders on second page and regulations relative to subletting service on star routes on third page of this circular.

Very respectfully,

W. S. Shallenberger

Second Assistant Postmaster General.

Mr. *Abram D. Hackman.*
Woodland Park
Teller Co.
Colo.

POST OFFICE WAS 29 YEARS YOUNG — This document awarded the post office mail route between South Park and Woodland Park from 1902 until 1906 to Abe Hackman, owner of the Midland Hotel and one of the early families. The first post office was established in 1873 while the area was still in El Paso County. This contract is dated two years after Woodland Park became part of Teller County.

This photograph was taken around 1900 from the southwest and shows the Colorado Midland Railway Eating House, with its distinctive mansard roof, on the north side of Midland Avenue. The next buildings include Creswell's Cafe, the Webb home, a blacksmith, the Baldwin store, and Creswell's Saloon. The long two-story building is N. W. Terrill's Dry Goods. The two-story building with the bell tower is the school. (UPHS, Wellington.)

The William Roberts family poses at their home west of Crystola and east of Woodland Park in 1921. Shown from left to right are Edith Lofland Roberts, Bessie Pearl, William Charles, Eudora Belva, and Freddie Roy. The 1915 cabin replaced the Junction House stage stop, which burned in 1912. The family sold the land and cabin on Crystola Road around 1938. (UPHS, Roberts.)

This is one of the original barns on the stagecoach line on Old Crystola Road, the original road into Woodland Park from the east. The Junction House was a way station for the stagecoaches. The stage stop, barns, and about 160 acres were part of the Ligon Ranch, later the Pinestone Ranch. The barns were torn down in a Chevy commercial around 1992. (UPHS.)

The Manitou Park Hotel was on land north of Woodland Park owned by Dr. William Bell, founder of Manitou Springs. He sold some of his property for homesteads and donated the rest to Colorado College for its School of Forestry. The college built this hotel, the third one on the site, in 1909. It was destroyed by fire on March 30, 1925. (UPHS; photograph by George and Zelma Worden.)

Dr. William Bell and Gen. William Palmer established the fish hatchery at Rainbow Falls, also known as Big Cold Spring, sometime after 1871. Before their enforced relocation by the treaty of 1880, the Utes used Big Cold Spring as a camping and hunting ground. Shown here in the 1920s, the hatchery and falls were later owned by Bob and Neva Watson from 1953 to 1990. (UPHS, Watson.)

A 1913 blizzard dumped more than 20 feet of snow on Bald Mountain and the surrounding area. This photograph was taken at the Gayler homestead on Bald Mountain east of Woodland Park on Rampart Range Road. Shown are, from left to right, Jack Gayler, schoolteacher Mary Blir, Irene Gayler, G. G. Gayler, Madge Mitts, and Stella Gayler. They used homemade skis to get around. (UPHS, Gayler.)

The Red Top Cabins in Woodland Park are shown in this Christmas greeting card from John and Clara Vos. This location at U.S. Highway 24 and the west side of Fairview Street has undergone numerous changes. The east side of Fairview was more stable, with a succession of names all used for the same building: Vos Antiques, Jerry's Junque, Paradise Café, the Martini Hut, and Liberty Bistro. (UPHS; photograph by Doris Breitenfeld.)

Here is the 640-acre Roberts family homestead north of Woodland Park in 1886. This cabin was replaced following a fire and the site later became the Thunderhead Inn casino in the 1950s. Behind the inn are the original barn, icehouse, and two cabins. Pictured from left to is the Roberts family: William, George, Addie, Roy, Hanna, Charles, and Elmer. (UPHS, Roberts.)

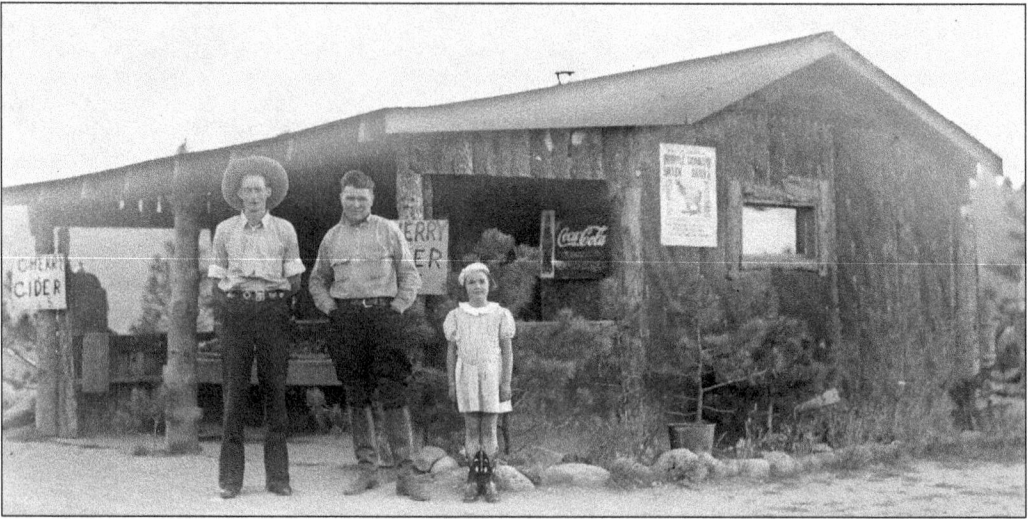

Shank (left), Nick Sanborn Sr., and Vera Sanborn Barnes are pictured at the store "above" Woodland Park, which likely meant the store was located on Bald Mountain, around 1931. The store was a convenient place to get supplies when the roads into Woodland Park were impassable. (UPHS, Barnes.)

This 1940 Woodland Park gas station was located at the northeast corner of Pine Street and Midland Avenue. The photograph was made into a Christmas greeting card. The station was built by Ira Woods (Woodland Park trustee 1932) and purchased by Otto Alcorn in 1940. Alcorn (WP trustee 1940 and 1941) is shown here with his three-year-old granddaughter Donna, later Donna Clifford. (UPHS, *Ute Pass Courier.*)

This is the Woodland Garage as it looked in 1949. It was located on the southwest corner of West Street and U.S. Highway 24 for about 40 years. Lucius Townsley, Alberta Townsley French's father, painted the sign for the garage. Note the acronym P.P.O.O. on the sign, which stands for the Pikes Peak Ocean to Ocean highway. These lots are now part of Our Lady of the Woods Roman Catholic Church. (UPHS, Townsley French.)

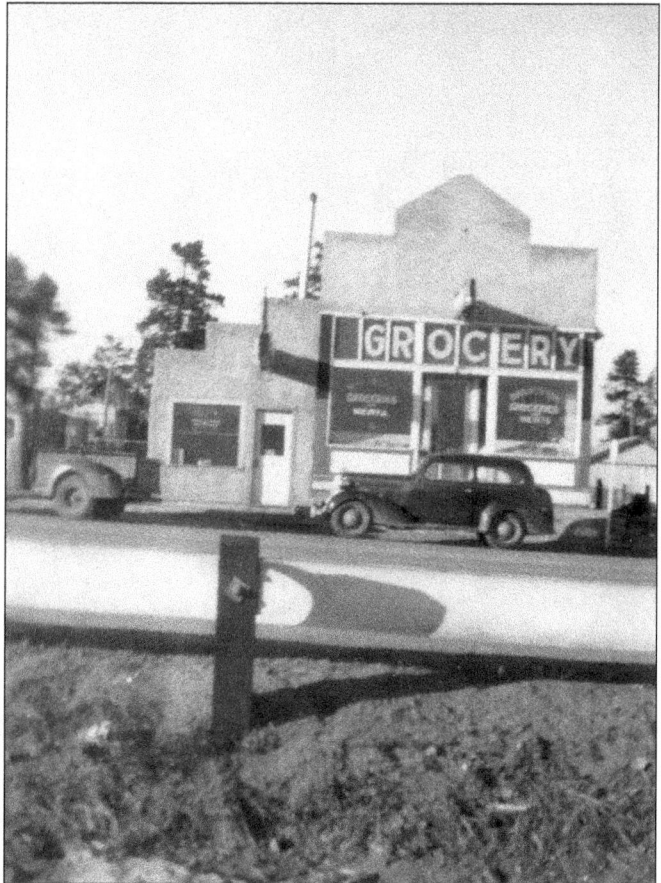

Graham's Grocery store at 216 West Midland Avenue, now U.S. Highway 24, was owned and operated by Ira Hollingsworth, who served as mayor as well as several terms as a trustee. Alva Cummins was the subsequent owner. He had previously worked as a butcher for John Carroll. The photograph is dated 1940. (UPHS, Barnes.)

31

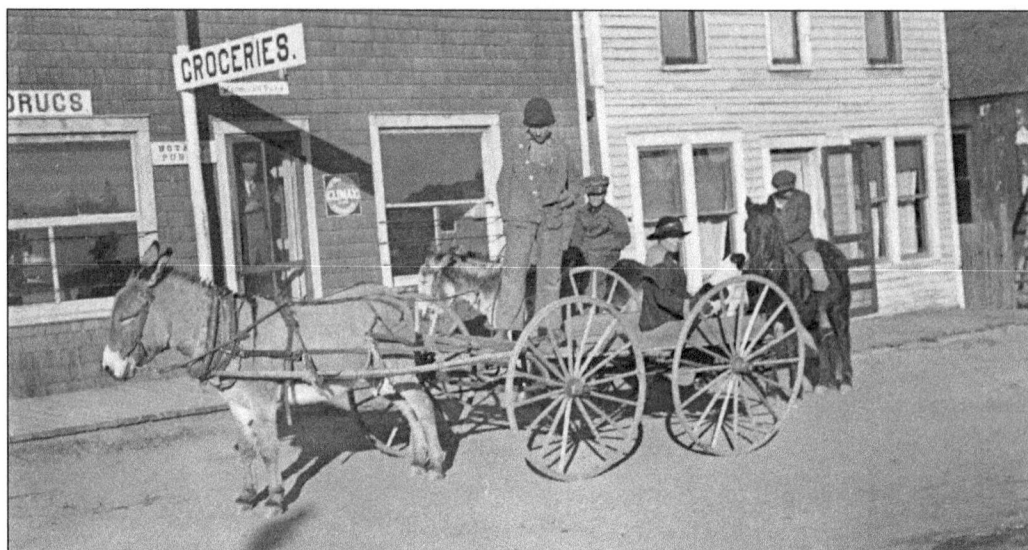

Hank Embree and an unidentified woman are shown on a wagon drawn by a burro in front of the drugstore and grocery store on Midland Avenue in the 1920s. Behind them are Bill Webb (left) and Richard Hachkman. In those days, there was a trip into town at least once a week to stock up on groceries. This could be quite an adventure, given the heavy snowfalls in the mountains. (UPHS; photograph by Mary Webb.)

Johnny Evans (center) rides with his companions in an early convertible in the 1930s in front on Carroll's Woodland Mercantile. Carroll's had the only telephone in town until the late 1920s. The Carrolls eventually added an extension to their home so they wouldn't have to go to the store in bad weather. John Carroll bought the mercantile from N. W. Terrill around 1898. (UPHS, H. H. Robinson.)

Mabel Middaugh and three unidentified children are pictured in the 1930s in front of Woodland Park's wooden sidewalks on Midland Avenue. Mabel was a widow at the time and worked at the school. She carried all the coal, carried out the ashes, cleaned the schoolrooms, and did all of the maintenance. (UPHS, H. H. Robinson.)

The calaboose was the jail built in July of 1891. The town paid McCulkey, Bright, and Bay $36.58 for labor and materials. It was originally located in the alley off Center Street, a half block from Midland Avenue. This photograph shows the calaboose in the parking lot across from Woodland Park City Hall in 1990. It was moved to its present location in History Park in 2009. (UPHS.)

H. H. Robinson built this stone, multi-office building on Midland Avenue in 1937. The post office is on the left, and Bert Bergstrom's Ute Bar is the last stone-front building on the right. Robinson came to Woodland Park in 1931. He built the Ouray Inn; installed the first cement sidewalks; ran a rustic furniture store with his wife, Marge; and had an arts and crafts shop. (UPHS, H. H. Robinson.)

Ira Rudy of Cascade is thought to have taken this 1886 photograph of the Free Methodist Church on the southwest corner of Park and Henrietta Streets. The image is unusual, with women pallbearers who appear to be dressed in matching dresses and bonnets in what appears to be a funeral procession. The decorations on the hearse do not seem to fit the occasion. (UPHS, Carroll.)

This was the first church in the Woodland Park area. Parishioners originally met in a hand-hewn log schoolhouse that was moved in 1890 to land donated by Henrietta Steffa. Most of the original structure is contained within the present building. After several additions and much remodeling, this building is still in existence, without the "His" and "Hers" doors on the east side. (UPHS, Carroll.)

This large log building was the home of sawmill owner George Sadler in the 1880s. The house was located on the Sadler ranch, located at the west end of what is now Evergreen Heights Drive. Sadler, who served as mayor of Woodland Park from 1912 to 1913 and as a trustee from 1913 to 1917, also owned a store, a livery, and other businesses in Divide. (UPHS, Walker.)

David Green built this house between 1891 and 1893 in the 600 block of Park Street. The original carriage house was behind the house. A guesthouse is next door to the main house, built at the same time. The front sidewalk permanently recorded the handprints of the Warren children when the Warren family moved there in 1968. (UPHS.)

This photograph of the Hackman House at 602 West Midland Avenue was taken by Frank Safranek in 1978. Andrew B. Hackman (Haachmann), a Dutch immigrant who homesteaded on Bald Mountain in the 1880s, built the house in 1897. The Hackman House later became an eating house, a boardinghouse, and a hotel. Today it is still a commercial venture, serving as a holistic wellness center. (UPHS, Safranek.)

This graceful home belonged to F. H. Woomer. He was the first Colorado Midland Railway stationmaster and the first mayor of Woodland Park. He was sworn-in on February 26, 1891. The house was later sold to Mrs. Richardson, who married Thomas Foster, a Woodland Park postmaster. It has since been known as the Foster Home. (UPHS, Roberts.)

Mr. and Mrs. Thomas Foster are shown on the porch of their home on the northwest corner of Elm Street and Midland Avenue with their four children, two burros, and one dog. The house was razed in 1986. Foster, a Woodland Park founding father, built homes in Green Mountain Falls and Woodland Park and is believed to have given Green Mountain Falls its name. (UPHS, H. H. Robinson.)

This was the home of John and Gertrude Carroll at West and Henrietta Streets as it appeared in 1989. The cabin was moved from the Paint Pony Ranch in the 1920s. The Embrees, Gertrude's family, added the curved arch over the front porch. Gertrude was a schoolteacher and the city's first postmistress. Since the 1990s, the cabin has housed Gary Litchenberg's Farmer's Insurance Agency. (UPHS.)

The Ladies Aid of the Woodland Park Church posed for a picture in 1923. In the first row from left to right are Lulu Townsley, Mame Carroll, Alice Turner with an unidentified child, Ruby Carroll, Margaret Carroll (the child), and three unidentified women. The women in the second row are unidentified. (UPHS, Townsley French.)

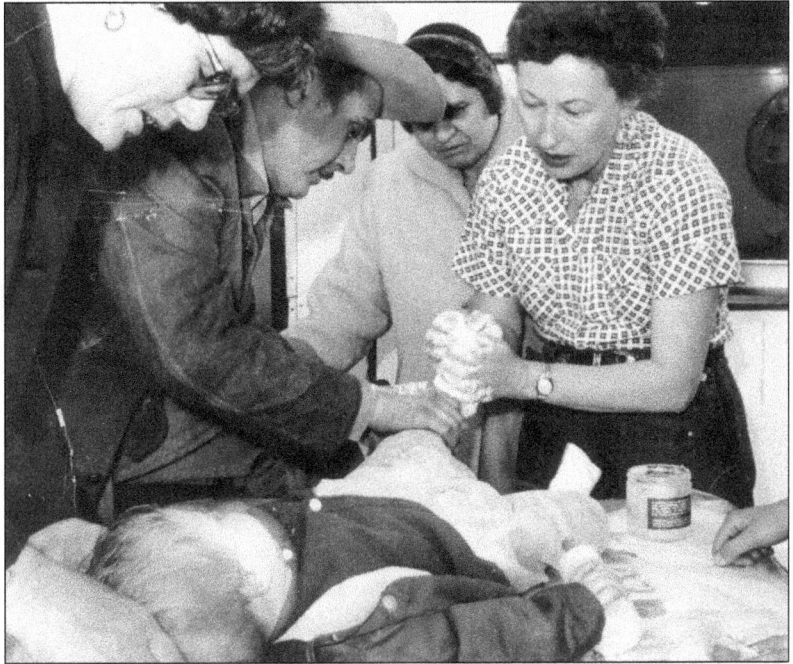

Alverta Burns, a nurse known as "angel of the hills," is shown treating a small patient. She and her husband bought the Triple B Ranch in 1947. There was no doctor in the area, so people brought patients to her in emergencies. She once disrupted a meal of about 50 guests to use the table to sew up the leg of a chainsaw accident victim. (UPHS, Burns.)

These four children posed for a photograph in front of their school in Crystola, a community located a little east of Woodland Park. When the rural schools in the area were consolidated in the 1920s, the Crystola School was merged with Woodland Park's school district. (UPHS, Musser.)

The Woodland Park School, located a mile west of Crystola, was built of hand-hewn logs around 1875 near the Silver Springs Ranch. Some of the children shown here were from the Roberts and Musser families. The Free Methodists also used the school for worship services. When it was no longer needed, the building was moved to Woodland Park to land owned by Henrietta Steffa. (UPHS, Lofland.)

Bessie, Eudora, and Fred Roberts are shown seated on the far left on the playground at Bald Mountain School, located on the mountain east and above Woodland Park. The other children are unidentified. Notice the handmade seesaw. Children's activities often relied on what was at hand and a rich imagination. (UPHS, Roberts.)

Among the children in this photograph, taken at Bald Mountain School in 1915, are Irene Gayler, Wallace Turner, Fred Roberts, and Jack Gayler. Les Gayler donated a half-acre of his land so the schoolhouse could be built. Children of this era generally had less free time and greater responsibilities than children today. They helped with farm and household chores or worked in their parents' businesses. (UPHS, Roberts.)

The Spielman School, located at Paint Pony Ranch just north of Woodland Park, is shown here in 1919. Fred Roberts is fifth from the right. Jane Bradford is the teacher. The other students are unidentified. Schools had to be in session just 60 days a year at that time. (UPHS, Roberts.)

This group photograph was taken in 1918. It shows teacher Gertie Flood with the school children at the Spielman School at the Paint Pony Ranch. Teachers' wages ranged from $35 to $75 per year for teaching all grades in a one-room school. (UPHS, Denny.)

Here is another group photograph of the students at the Spielman School. This one was taken in 1919. Most schools had only seven grades and received state or county funding if a licensed teacher taught the children. Textbooks were free. Notice that all of the girls are in skirts and most of the boys are wearing hats and ties. (UPHS, Roberts.)

The children of the Spielman School pose in front of their bus on a winter day. Early school buses were often converted from trucks and had no heat. Winter temperatures in this part of the mountains can dip to 10 or 15 degrees below zero, and blizzards can occur from October until May. (UPHS, Elene Spielman.)

This two-story frame schoolhouse was built east of Fairview Avenue and north of Midland Avenue in 1890 and housed grades one through twelve. In 1927, a second building was moved from Edlowe west of Woodland Park and placed next door. In 1939, a new building with four classrooms and a gymnasium was completed. The gymnasium building is now the Ute Pass Cultural Center. (UPHS, Carroll.)

The pupils of the Woodland Park School posed for this photograph in April 1925. The PTA sponsored square dances at the school every other week. Some of the teachers there in the 1930s and 1940s included Olin Little, George Worden, Ruby Thompson, Estelle Rodgers, Jo Wondergem, Kate Eiswerth, and Lowell Cook. (UPHS, Howard and Martha Webb.)

The Woodland Park schoolyard is shown here with a new building under construction in 1932. The small building in front is the newer school, housing grades one through three. The original, two-story school building housed the upper grades. On the left is Marge Robinson. Marge's grandmother, Mabel Middaugh, was a school custodian. (UPHS, H. H. Robinson.)

Woodland Park High School students pose in front of the building in 1943. It became the middle school and was later restored for use as the Ute Pass Cultural Center. From left to right are (first row) unidentified, Fern Kowitz, two unidentified, and Jimmy Johns; (second row) Nancy Woods, unidentified, Dolores Sater, and Iris Wilkie. (UPHS, H. H. Robinson.)

This train engine is thought to be the engine from the "No Name Railroad." It operated north of Woodland Park to transport logs from Dr. William Bell's property to the Lions Camp. This narrow-gauge railroad was likely the first logging railroad in Colorado. It was apparently hauled up Ute Pass in parts on wagons drawn by teams of oxen or mules. (UPHS.)

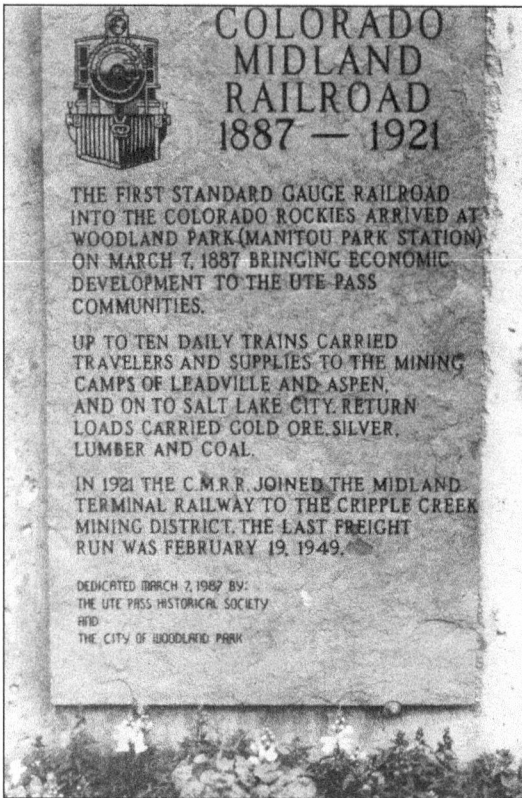

COLORADO
MIDLAND
RAILROAD
1887 — 1921

THE FIRST STANDARD GAUGE RAILROAD
INTO THE COLORADO ROCKIES ARRIVED AT
WOODLAND PARK (MANITOU PARK STATION)
ON MARCH 7, 1887 BRINGING ECONOMIC
DEVELOPMENT TO THE UTE PASS
COMMUNITIES.

UP TO TEN DAILY TRAINS CARRIED
TRAVELERS AND SUPPLIES TO THE MINING
CAMPS OF LEADVILLE AND ASPEN,
AND ON TO SALT LAKE CITY. RETURN
LOADS CARRIED GOLD ORE, SILVER,
LUMBER AND COAL.

IN 1921 THE C.M.R.R. JOINED THE MIDLAND
TERMINAL RAILWAY TO THE CRIPPLE CREEK
MINING DISTRICT. THE LAST FREIGHT
RUN WAS FEBRUARY 19, 1949.

DEDICATED MARCH 7, 1987 BY:
THE UTE PASS HISTORICAL SOCIETY
AND
THE CITY OF WOODLAND PARK

This Colorado Midland Railway memorial marker is in Bergstrom Park. This was the first standard-gauge railroad to cross the continental divide. It was incorporated in 1884. In 1887, the first train ran from Colorado Springs to Leadville, bringing prosperity and a sense of purpose to the region for the next 60 years. The photograph was taken in 1987. (UPHS, Lackman.)

A group poses at the original Colorado Midland Station in Woodland Park around 1900. On the left are Edwin and Mabel Middaugh. The two women on the right are unidentified. The railroad carried passengers, gold and silver ore, lumber, and produce. By 1895, the Midland Terminal Railroad was shipping gold ore from Cripple Creek through Divide to Colorado Springs via the Colorado Midland Railway. (UPHS, H. H. Robinson.)

Midland Terminal engine No. 63 is seen in the late 1940s at Woodland Park's third and final train station. By 1918, through a series of local and national political maneuvers, the Colorado Midland Railway went into receivership. The Midland Terminal Railroad acquired track, equipment, and facilities from Divide to Colorado Springs and continued to operate until 1949, carrying gold ore, mail, cattle, lumber, and produce. (UPHS, Gillaspy.)

This was the second Colorado Midland Railway station in Woodland Park. The Hackman Livery barn is shown behind the station on the left. The Midland Hotel is in the background on the right. The station was built in 1904 and burned down in 1935. The baggage room portion, which didn't burn, was moved to Memorial Park and became known as Memorial Hall. (UPHS, Carroll.)

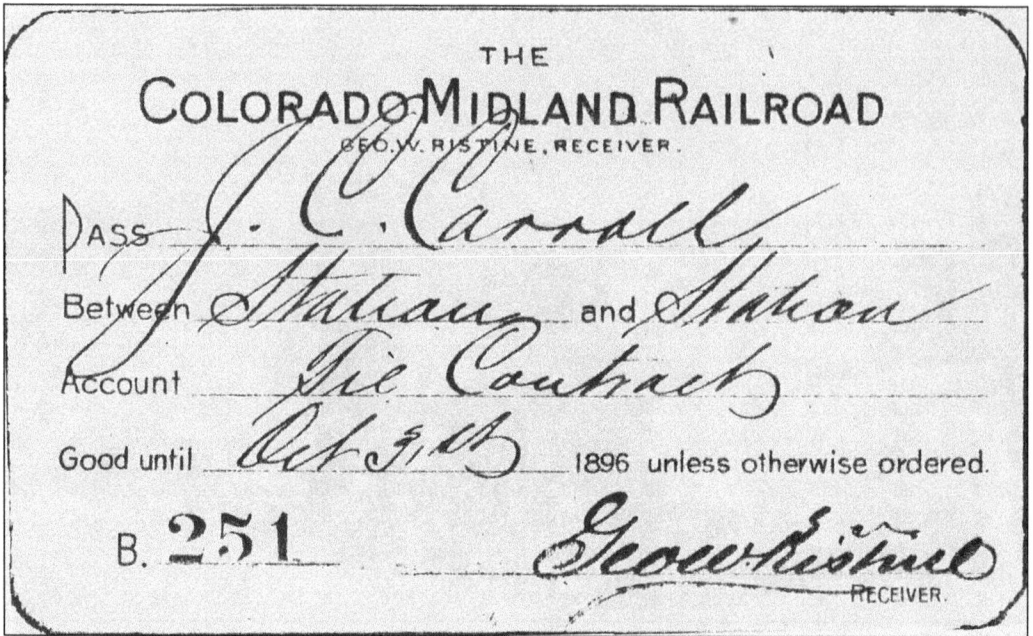

Here is a copy of a Colorado Midland Railroad pass issued to John C. Carroll and good until October 31, 1896. He was a railroad tie contractor for the railway line. It is signed by George W. Ristine, receiver. A few years later, John Carroll bought and operated the former N. W. Terrill mercantile store at Woodland Park. (UPHS, Carroll.)

The Colorado Midland Railway Band provided popular entertainment at many different venues, as seen here on September 29, 1917. The first time they tried to play at the Summit House on Pikes Peak, they couldn't get enough air. Stephen Fagin is the second bass (tuba) from left. The Colorado Midland Railway also sponsored a women's chorale, the Midland Merry Maids. (UPHS, Fagin.)

The former baggage room of the Colorado Midland Railway station is seen here in 2004 as the Clothes Closet. After the rest of the station burned, it was moved to Memorial Park on the northeast corner of Center and Henrietta Streets. Memorial Hall was the first Woodland Park Public Library briefly in the mid-1960s. It was used as the Clothes Closet for about eight years. (UPHS.)

One of last runs of the Midland Terminal Railroad was photographed west of Woodland Park. This train is about 100 yards west of the intersection of Trout Creek Road and U.S. Highway 24. It is just clearing a 16-degree curve on its way toward the Lynch ranch on South Forty Road. Mary Heltemes took pictures of the train in February 1949. (UPHS, Heltemes.)

The Midland Terminal Railroad is seen here in its last week of service in February 1949. The train stopped operating because gold ore processing mills had been built in Cripple Creek and the rich ore played out. This ended the need to transport the ore to the mill in Colorado Springs. Ironically, the train brought in parts for the Cripple Creek mills. (UPHS, Heltemes.)

A Midland Terminal train chugs past the Lynch Ranch parallel to the South Forty Road. The train route west out of Woodland Park followed what is now U.S. Highway 24 past the Trout Creek Road traffic light and then turned to the southeast and south instead of going up Bluebird Hill. (UPHS, Lynch.)

Midland Terminal engine No. 64 steams through Woodland Park on January 22, 1949. Notice the two additional engines in back pushing the load up the steep grade through Ute Pass. On the downhill run through the lower part of the pass below Woodland Park, there were several derailments, washouts, and at least one runaway train. (UPHS, Gillaspy.)

One of last runs of the Midland Terminal Railroad was recorded in this February 1949 image from Woodland Park. The last run of the Midland Terminal was recorded by KRDO radio of Colorado Springs. The recording includes interviews with the train crew and some of the last whistles heard before the train went silent after 62 years of service. (UPHS, Heltemes.)

The Lowell Thomas Special of the Midland Terminal Railroad took place on January 27, 1949. It stopped in Woodland Park on the way to Cripple Creek. Lowell Thomas was the guest of honor for one of these. The famous news reporter, commentator, and world traveler (who grew up in Victor and the Cripple Creek District) was joined by boxer Jack Dempsey (also native to the district) for the occasion. The Rocky Mountain Railroad Club chartered the train on February 6, 1949, and according to Lowell Thomas, "The engine's mournful whistle echoed off the canyon walls playing the Requiem for the last railroad into the 'World's Greatest Gold Camp.'" Engine No. 59 pulled several of the last runs of the Midland Terminal. Toward the close of its operation, the railroad had almost entirely stopped carrying regular passenger traffic. About a year later, February 19, 1950, the engine whistle blew for the last time and was reported by local residents from Manitou to Cripple Creek. (UPHS, Mr. and Mrs. L. Thole.)

Three

FROM FOREST TO SAWMILL TO GOLD MINE

At first, logging was simply a necessity for ranchers who required timber for their homes, stock pens, barns, and fences. It became an industry after the newly redesigned Ute Pass Road opened up along Fountain Creek in 1872, and loggers were able to provide building material for Old Colorado City, Colorado Springs, and Manitou Springs. By 1881, thousands of logs were being shipped on 8 miles of rail on the No Name Railroad, which ran from property north of present-day Woodland Park that was owned William Bell, to the sawmills that dotted the area. From there, milled lumber was loaded onto wagons and sent to Colorado Springs.

With the arrival of the Colorado Midland Railway, production was stepped up to more than a million board feet of lumber and 200,000 railroad ties per year. The railroad also provided lumber transport to the city of Cripple Creek, which needed as much milled wood as it could get to accommodate the phenomenal growth that accompanied the gold rush of the 1890s. Woodland Park also provided the milled lumber that Cripple Creek needed to rebuild following the devastating fires of 1896, as well as the wood the town of Victor would need following a major fire there in 1899.

With the creation of the Pike Timber Reserve in February of 1892 and the Pike National Forest in 1906, forest rangers were responsible for approving the harvesting of trees. As late as 1936, some 20,000 railroad ties a year were still being cut, milled, and dipped in boiling creosote in Woodland Park near the center of town. Sam and Bert Dilts and Jake Workman operated the largest mills in town. All the mills were steam powered. Some were portable, steam-driven mills with wood boilers that were moved from gulch to gulch as each area was logged.

This sawmill operated in Woodland Park in 1890. It stood at the east end of Midland Avenue and on the north side of Colorado Midland tracks and was owned by George Sadler (and briefly, A. B. Hackman). For most of the time, Bert and Sam Dilts operated it. These mills were producing thousands of railroad ties and timber props for the mines. Four to six other mills operated in Woodland Park in 1890. Jake Workman owned one of these, located south of Midland Avenue, east of Fairview. According to Les Mulnix, Workman's mill was considered a real eyesore. The Sadler mill was located about where the Prudential Building is today. Former occupants of the lots were the Snake Pit, Browncraft Restaurant, China Cabin Restaurant, and Austin's Restaurant. (UPHS, Roberts.)

In 1921, Lloyd Stoner and his father established a sawmill at Midland. In 1934, the mill burned, forcing them to start over again. At first they both cut and milled timber, but later they focused only on milling. In 1928, they began transporting lumber by truck because of the increasing cost of shipping by rail. This photograph shows Lloyd Stoner with lumbering equipment on March 21, 1978. (UPHS, Stoner.)

Lloyd Stoner Sr. is pictured here in his lumberyard with a horse-drawn lumber wagon. Sawmills had been busy for decades. Joe Sales had his mill in Ute Park (Chipita Park), a man named French ran one at French Creek, H. C. Childs ran mills at Crystola and Silver Springs Ranch, and Charlie Walker had a portable mill, which was moved to Manitou Park in 1875. So profitable was the lumber industry that by 1874, the U.S. Forest Service was patrolling for "timber trespassers." (UPHS, Stoner.)

Here is another photograph of Lloyd Stoner's lumber mill at Midland, this one taken in 1926, five years after the mill was established. Shown from left to right are Lloyd Stoner; Frank Wellington (a forest ranger who built trails for lumbering); Ralph Cahill; Lionel "Bud" Wellington (Frank's son); and Alfred Cole. (UPHS, Stoner.)

Lloyd Stoner Sr. is shown in this photograph with an unidentified employee at Stoner's Midland lumber mill in 1947. By this time, the once-lucrative lumbering industry in Woodland Park was beginning to show signs of slowing down. Stoner Sr. died two years later, at the age of 74. (UPHS, Stoner.)

FREIGHT BILL

This is the paid receipt for a freight bill, dated January 24, 1924. It indicates the amount charged, $63.27, for 5,500 pounds of mine timbers to Portland Mine Company by Midland Terminal Railway Company Mine timbers were transported from Divide to Victor-Bullhill on Midland Terminal No. 45. D. P. Fleming was the railway agent. (UPHS, Idoux.)

Edwin Armentrout was Pike National Forest ranger for Cascade, Green Mountain Falls, and Chipita Park in the 1920s and 1930s. He was Anna May Wellington Armentrout's husband. The Armentrouts were among the 12 families who had a homestead of 160 acres each on Bald Mountain. (UPHS, Wellington.)

Edwin Armentrout is shown on a horse around 1900. The Armentrouts and Wellingtons had a number of ranches in the Ute Pass area. One Wellington homestead was located along the north side of Highway 24 just after the gravel pit and before the east entrance to Green Mountain Falls. (UPHS, Wellington.)

The Colorado College School of Forestry at Manitou Park students are shown here in 1924. The school was established in 1906 on 10,635 acres donated by Gen. William Palmer and Dr. William Bell. The forestry school closed in 1934, and the property was turned over to the U.S. Forest Service to be used as a demonstration forest. It was expanded in 1936 to include 16,560 acres. (UPHS, Townsley French.)

This Brotherhood Gold Mining and Milling Certificate was issued to L. M. Frank for 78,000 shares, dated July 20, 1900, and signed by H. C. Childs, secretary, and M. H. Leddy, president. Childs and other Spiritualists believed that gold would be found in Crystola Canyon. Shafts and mine exploration holes were dug throughout the area, but nothing much was ever found. In the meantime, they built a mill, erected a solid-rock-wall building (in which to store the gold), founded a town, sold lots for cabins, and opened a store. Later on, professors and others affiliated with Colorado College started building cabins and having summer gatherings and retreats there. The canyon became known as "College Gulch," until one night in the late 1920s, when the fishing dam broke. The flood of water swept away many of the cabins, and one person died. Parts of the area are now back in the national forest, and a few lots are still occupied by cabin-owners taking advantage of 99-year leases. (UPHS, Morrow.)

The Lettie H. Gold Mining Company, located in Woodland Park and incorporated on November 24, 1902, reported a capitalization of $1 million. Officers were president Jo C. Griffith; vice president George E. Powell; secretary John C. Carroll; treasurer Irvin R. Fry; and manager H. D. Hackman. The mine's prospectus promised a significant return on investment, but the mine produced little gold. (UPHS Collection.)

The
Lettie H.
Gold Mining
Company

Properties in Teller Co., Colo.

PRINCIPAL OFFICE AT
WOODLAND PARK
TELLER COUNTY, COLO.

Incorporated Nov. 24th, 1902

Capitalization, $1,000,000

Par Value per Share, $1.00
Full Paid and Non-assessable

OFFICERS AND DIRECTORS:
JO. C. GRIFFITH, - - - - - - President
GEO. E. POWELL, - - - - Vice President
JOHN C. CARROLL, - - - - - Secretary
IRVIN F. FRY
H. D. HACKMAN, - - - Treasurer and Manager

This photograph shows the site of the Lettie H. Mine in 1990 on Gold Hill near U.S. Highway 24 and Trout Creek Road. This dig is on the northwest face of Gold Hill and looks little different than the scene of hundreds of other such attempts to find gold in the area surrounding Woodland Park. (UPHS.)

This limestone outcropping near Westcreek was thought by some to be one of George Pemberton's "salted" mines in the area. Mines were salted by loading gold nuggets or powder into a shotgun shell and firing them into a likely place to fool buyers and investors into thinking they had discovered gold. This photograph was taken in 1989. (UPHS.)

This abandoned mine is located on the ridge just west of the Shining Mountain golf course and Rule Creek, north of Woodland Park. It is on the east edge of 120 acres formerly known as the "salted mine" property. One of the Spur 717 trails crossed the ridge close to the mine. It is on private property now. This photograph was taken in 2000. (UPHS, Parkhurst.)

This photograph shows Fisher's Lumber Camp in the early 1880s. The current-day location of the camp's south end is just north of where Forest Road 342 splits into Lions Camp Road and Templed Hills Road. The track, rolling stock, and all other equipment was brought up the Ute Pass wagon road on wagons drawn by teams of oxen and mules. (UPHS.)

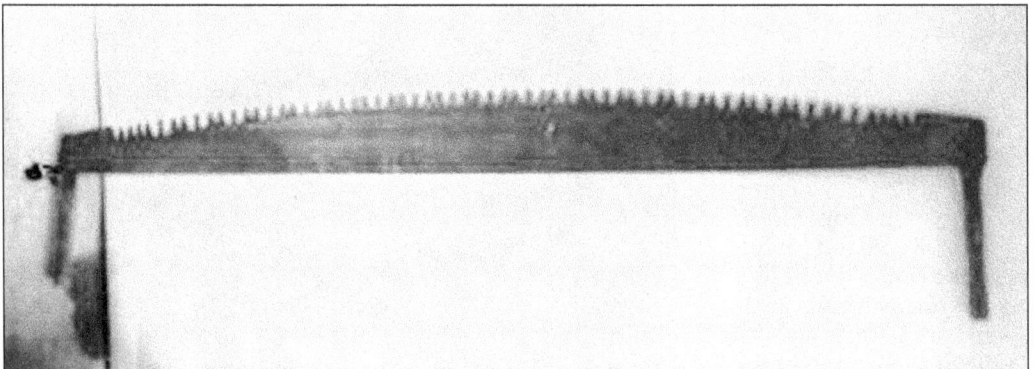

Francis Allen Hart donated this two-man saw used by lumbermen and carpenters to cut wood for cabins for the summer tourists. Wood was used for heating and cooking in the summer. It was used as recently as 1960. This is one of thousands of objects and photographs donated to the society by its founding members. (UPHS, Hart.)

This homemade snag-toothed saw, shown here with its case, was used to cut trees for home fires and lumber. This saw was made and used by Martin Hammer. He had all the specialized equipment—like finger chains, rough chains, and figure-eight chains—to get logs out of the forest with a team. (UPHS, Hammer.)

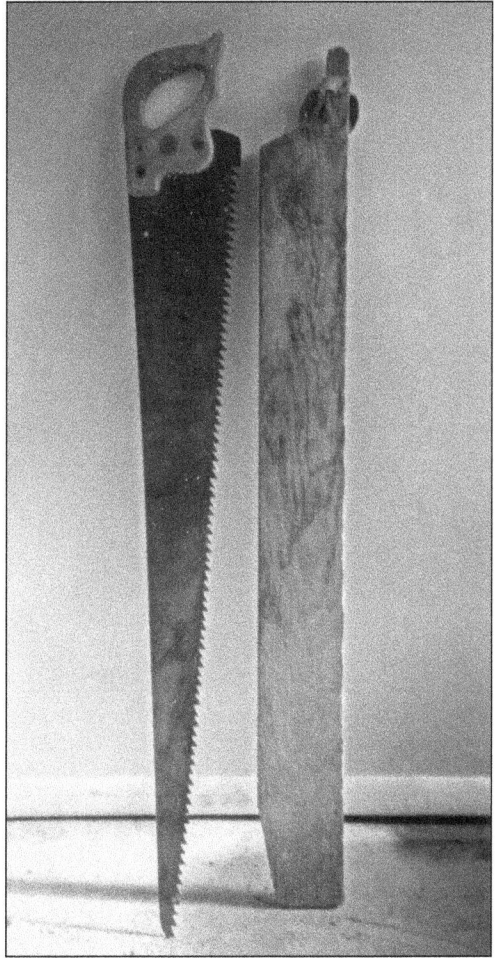

Ice saws were vital pieces of 19th-century equipment. Towns with lakes harvested and stored ice to use for refrigeration during the summer. In the mid-1930s, the Colorado State Health Department ordered Woodland Park to stop using lake water for drinking. This created a hardship for residents accustomed to chopping holes in the ice at Memorial Park Lake to get water when their pipes froze. (UPHS, LaHaye.)

The K. W. Quinn home in Crystola was on the Ute Pass Historical Society Home Tour in 1978, the year this photograph was taken. The house is on the site of an old cyanide mill owned by the Victory Gold Extraction Company and known as the Crystola Cyanide Mill. (UPHS, Safranek.)

The Crystola Cyanide Mill (Victory Gold Extraction Company) was in existence from 1901 to 1914. The mill was built by Henry C. Childs and fellow Spiritualists in response to a revelation that gold was to be found in Crystola. It marked the beginning of one of the biggest stock-selling schemes in Colorado history. This is a copy of a newspaper photograph. (UPHS.)

Henry C. Childs, former speaker of the Illinois House of Representatives, came to Colorado on the advice of a seer in 1872. He founded the town of Crystola, entertained mediums, held séances, built a laboratory, and studied metallurgy and mineralogy. The publication *Ores and Metals* credits Childs with discovering gold in Cripple Creek in 1878. Expecting to discover gold on his Crystola property, he built a stone structure to store his gold. (UPHS, Morrow.)

This barn, photographed in 1991, can still be seen in Crystola. Many believe it was built from lumber originally used to build the Victory Gold Extraction Company mill in Crystola. Some of the old-timers say that this barn was built over the foundation of the stone house where Henry Childs planned to store his gold. (UPHS.)

This cabin on Mule Creek is located on property now owned by the U.S. Forest Service. Historians believe that the site may once have been part of Skelton Ranch. This view is from the southeast. There is a 40-foot horizontal mine shaft about 150 feet north of the cabin. (UPHS, Parkhurst.)

Alberta Townsley (French) is shown at a mine on Bald Mountain east of Woodland Park in 1920. Her husband, Bill French, remembers that the gold mine never seemed to "hit it." (The ore was worth only about $20 per ton.) Alberta's father was a painter, paperhanger, and sign painter, and did much of the painting and decorating in town. (UPHS, Townsley French.)

Four

HERE COME THE TOURISTS

With the improvement of the road between Colorado Springs and Ute Pass in the 1880s and the arrival of the Colorado Midland Railway in Woodland Park in March 1887, tourism was working its way up to the town. Fine hotels were built in the towns on the way up to Woodland Park, and the area was becoming known as a summer resort. The first hotel in Woodland Park was the Crest Hotel, a frame building with 15 rooms, which was built in 1889 at the corner of Park and Lake Avenues. A pavilion was located up the hill behind the hotel and became a popular picnic spot in the 1890s.

A larger hotel, the 42-room Woodland Hotel, was built in 1892. Behind it was a baseball diamond whose stands were filled with spectators who rode the train from Colorado Springs to see the Western League games that were banned in Colorado Springs on Sundays. When Colorado Springs left the league, the visitors from Colorado Springs diminished, and the hotel declined. It became a tuberculosis sanitarium during the 1920s and was torn down in the 1930s.

The railroad company built the Colorado Midland Eating House, which later became a Harvey House restaurant and even later was moved across the street from the railroad station to become the Midland Hotel. It was the busiest hotel in the area and the only one open year-round. It was torn down in the early 1940s.

Over the years, Woodland Park has served as a junction for travel to other locations and continues to be a business center and a year-round town. Summer camps, dude ranches, and outdoor activities are favored attractions in the surrounding area.

Dickinson and Marble built Crest Hotel in 1884. It was a prefabricated building of 15 rooms assembled on the northeast corner of Park and Lake Streets. It had a parlor, dining room, and kitchen on the first floor, bedrooms upstairs, and no bathrooms. In 1902, Mrs. James Green ran the hotel. It was razed in 1910. The lumber was used to build homes in town. (UPHS, Carroll.)

The Woodland Hotel, opened in 1893, had 55 rooms—42 of which were bedrooms. The hotel also featured a dining room, two kitchens, a lobby, two parlors, a circular stairway, and four indoor bathrooms. Kitchens and stables were behind the hotel. John Anisfield of Ohio contracted for the hotel to be built by J. W. Bell. They were issued a building permit January 1, 1892, to construct the hotel for a price of $15,000. (UPHS.)

In 1892, A. B. Hackman bought the closed Midland Eating House, moved it across the street, remodeled the upstairs, and turned it into the Midland Hotel. Ruby Carroll said the Midland was the busiest hotel in the area and the only one open year-round. It never had indoor plumbing, but it was known for serving wonderful meals. This photograph was taken around 1935. The building was razed in 1942 or 1943. (UPHS, Carroll Collection.)

The first Manitou Hotel was built in 1873 at Dr. Bell's Manitou Park and Ranch. It burned in 1887. This photograph shows the second hotel, which itself burned just before the start of the tourist season in 1889. It was a three-story hotel, built with locally cut lumber. A third hotel was built in 1909 by Colorado College. It burned down in 1925. (UPHS, George and Velma Worden.)

SKELTON'S SUMMER

RANCH RESORT

A

PICTURESQUE VILLAGE

OF

LOG CABINS

AND

CANVAS TOPPED COTTAGES.

3½ MILES FROM WOODLAND PARK

ON THE

COLORADO MIDLAND R'Y.

RATES, $3.00 PER DAY.

SPECIAL RATE FOR THOSE SPENDING

A MONTH OR MORE.

LOCATION.

Skelton's Mountain Ranch consists of 2,000 acres, situated in Ute Pass, three and one-half miles from the ranch station on the Colorado Midland R. R., nineteen miles from Manitou, twenty-five miles from Colorado Springs and one hundred miles from Denver.

The elevation is over 7,000 feet.

The surroundings are wild and picturesque, with Pike's Peak in full view at a distance of ten miles.

At hand are Nature's grandest features of high peaks, rugged country, beautiful glens, clear mountain streams, forest and valley to lend charm to walk and drive.

PIKE'S PEAK FROM DINING HALL

ACCOMMODATIONS.

Comfort is guaranteed you in these wild surroundings. Guests are accommodated in log cabins or roomy canvas cottages, having floors, screens and ample furnishings. They are heated on cool evenings and supplied with pure spring water.

Mineral springs are within easy walking distance.

This photograph shows two pages of the Skelton Ranch brochure. This ranch was about 3 miles west of Woodland Park. William T. and Lizzie Skelton acquired land starting in 1905 that later became the Skelton Ranch. It was a resort and a dude ranch, the first in the area. Skelton was a district judge from St. Louis and a Colorado Springs lawyer who became a Colorado Springs judge. He was one of the early homesteaders in the area and eventually acquired about 1600 acres. The judge was known to be a genial host. There appears to have been one main lodge with large fireplaces at each end of the living room. There were a number of cabins, each with their own fireplace. There were also several canvas-topped cottages. The remains indicate at least one large three-story barn and stables featuring concrete-lined floors and walls. The ranch offered meals, mountain climbing, fishing, horseback riding, and wagon trips to Pikes Peak and Colorado Springs. (UPHS, Glen and Barbara Garner.)

A fine rustic dining hall built of logs, containing two large fireplaces, accommodates 200 guests. Across a gulch, spanned by a rustic bridge, is a commodious log assembly hall for entertainments.

Good meals are guaranteed, including poultry, fresh eggs and vegetables, the products of the ranch.

The ranch herd of fine cows furnishes an abundance of pure milk, cream and butter.

AGREEABLE PEOPLE.

The patronage of refined people only is solicited, that guests may be sure of meeting only

VERANDA OF DINING HALL.

agreeable people in the informal life of this mountain resort.

DIVERSIONS.

Weekly trips will be made at request to Pike's Peak and to Cripple Creek on horseback or by wagon.

Daily picnic excursions if desired may be made, with guides, to interesting points by mountain wagon, on horseback or burros.

Two (free) excursions on the ranch each week.

The ranch itself furnishes points of interest for daily trips to fill a month, many of them in easy walking distance.

Mountain climbing, fishing in the streams, walks, drives, or lazy days in hammock and shade, suit all who like "outdoors."

FOR HEALTH.

Rest is change. From city and work the ranch offers the relief of pure air, pure water,

SIGHTSEEING FROM THE SADDLE.

pleasant outdoor occupation, with no mud, no mosquitoes, no hay fever, asthma or kindred diseases.

For further information address

W. T. SKELTON, Manager,

"Skelton Mountain Ranch,"

Woodland Park, Colorado.

These are photographs of contiguous pages of a Skelton Ranch brochure, which boasts, "The ranch produces hay, oats, wheat, barley, and rye in amazing quantities per acre in addition to potatoes, cabbage, beets, and all kinds of vegetables in unsurpassed amounts and quality." The brochure also notes, "Gold ore has been discovered on the ranch of the same formation that has made Cripple Creek famous…. Ranch gold ore is now discovered assaying from $9.55 to $1020.42 per ton." The ranch operated for about 15 years from approximately 1906 until the early 1920s when Judge Skelton died. Lizzie Skelton died in March of 1942. The federal government purchased the land in September 1939. (UPHS, Glen and Barbara Garner.)

This is a view of the Skelton Ranch taken in 1989 just outside Woodland Park, north of Trout Creek Road. The remains of the fireplace from the ranch's main lodge can still be found today at the ranch site. There is a hiking trail nearby. (UPHS; photograph by Bob Horn.)

This 2002 photograph highlights the scenic, forested area where the Skelton Ranch was located. Horseback riding was the favorite activity of visitors in those days and would have been a great adventure for city folks. The small hill in the middle at the horizon is on the west side of Gold Hill. Note the antennae on the top of the hill. (UPHS; photograph by Hintz.)

The Colorado Midland Railway offered Wildflower Excursions from 1912 to 1919. This photograph shows a car in Woodland Park. On Thursdays, the train left Colorado Springs, traveling through Ute Pass to Florissant and 11 Mile Canyon, where passengers spent mornings picking wildflowers and afternoons digging fossils at Florissant fossil beds. The Midland ceased operations west of Divide in 1919. (Brigham University.)

• Scenic Sylvan Resort Invites Vacationists •

WOODLAND PARK, COLORADO

VIEW OF THE NORTH SLOPE OF PIKES PEAK FROM WOODLAND PARK

BIRDSEYE VIEW OF WOODLAND PARK FROM SURROUNDING HILLS

VIEW OF THE NEW PAVED HIGHWAY (U.S. 24) TO WOODLAND PARK FROM COLORADO SPRINGS

Taken From 1938 Tourist Edition Of Colorado Springs Gazette And Telegraph

This 1938 article in the Tourist Edition of the *Colorado Springs Gazette Telegraph* describes the Scenic Sylvan Resort, inviting vacationers to Woodland Park. Resorts like this flourished in the 1920s and 1930s. The town is still a popular getaway, a very scenic resort area with many outdoor activities.

Paradise Ranch

The Paradise Ranch was owned and operated by Frank and Lavera Snell from 1928 until it was sold in 1970. A group from Texas operated it for the next five years. Frank Snell (right) is shown here in about 1965 with one of the stagecoaches in his collection. The Karsten Corporation bought the lodge and the land in the late 1980s with the vision of developing a subdivision called Paradise Estates. (UPHS.)

This photograph shows how the Paradise Lodge looked in 1989. The lodge was reopened for a brief period as the Settlement House Restaurant. The Paradise Ranch Restaurant, Saloon, and Lodge opened in late 1988. Dieter and Patricia Seilbold, Kathy Wilson, and Jerry Stuhlsatz then owned it. The Seilbolds also owned the Swiss Chalet. Robert Cochran was the chef at both the Swiss and Paradise. (UPHS.)

This photograph shows the Paradise Dude Ranch in 1965. The main lodge, guest quarters, swimming pool, guest cabins, staff cabins, and housing for female staff were on the north side of Highway 24. The rodeo grounds, barns, the collection of wagons, stages, buggies, bunkhouse for the wranglers, and even a chariot from the movie *Ben Hur* were located south of the highway in the current-day Safeway Plaza area. (UPHS.)

This old chimney and a small concrete slab is all that remains of some unknown structure on the present Paradise Estates property. About 100 feet to the north and east is a cement blockhouse cistern used to collect water from springs farther up toward Rampart Range. This is one of six chimneys and other structures remaining from the Paradise Ranch days. (UPHS, Hintz.)

This is a Tally-Ho wagon from Paradise Ranch. It would bring ranch guests into Woodland Park for sightseeing excursions. The ranch hired 150 employees and another 25 wranglers and bought strings of horses for the summer season. It was a very popular dude ranch in the 1950s, with the guests returning year after year. (UPHS, Zoe Davis.)

This is a photograph of Poncho's grave site on the old Paradise Dude Ranch. It says on the marker, "Poncho, Mrs. Snell's beloved stallion." The legend is that Poncho, who belonged to Lavera Snell, was buried standing up with his silver-adorned bridle and saddle. His grave is about 200 yards north by northwest of the intersection of Kings Crown Road and Kings Crown Road. (UPHS, Hintz.)

This photograph is of Vince Gordon's log house. It was built in the 1930s as a summer cabin but has been enlarged and remodeled since then. Vince Gordon is a past mayor of Woodland Park. Many summer cabins were built during the 1930s; escaping to the mountains was a favorite pastime then and remains one today. (UPHS.)

This is the Park Hotel in 1989. It is the former 1930s La Fonda Hotel at the southeast corner of Park and Henrietta Streets. A lot of building went on during the 1930s to accommodate vacationers looking for a cool, interesting place to stay in the mountains. The location was convenient, as it was not far from the city, but still gave visitors the feeling of getting away. (UPHS.)

This picture was taken at the Quarter Circle H Dude Ranch for Girls. It was started by Lee Hermann and his wife, Gus, and continued by Rick Hermann (center) and his wife, Til (sixth from the left), with their son and daughter, Curt and Fredi (right front row), until about 1955. The camp was coed when it started in the 1930s, for 18-to-21-year-olds from the East Coast. In the 1940s, it was just for girls, as boys were otherwise occupied with World War II. It was located north of Woodland Park on the Rampart Range Road. The Hermanns later also ran the boys' dude ranch called Silver Spur, located about 4 miles west of Woodland Park on Highway 24 on the south side of the road. These were both working ranches with 200 horses, cattle, lumbering, and haying. When the teens arrived for the summer, they helped the Hermanns, along with about 30 staff. Part of the site is today the home of Red and Ruth Williams. (UPHS, Robin Spaulding.)

When this photograph was taken in 2005, this building was Austin's Restaurant. It is now the Prudential Building. It was the original site of the Sadler lumber mill. Later the Dilts, Sam and Burt, ran the mill for about 25 years. The lot was the site of the Snake Pit, the Browncraft Restaurant, and the China Cabin. The Snake Pit was a tourist attraction featuring live snakes. (UPHS, Hintze.)

This building on Fairview Street between Midland Avenue and Highway 24 has served as home to many businesses. It was Vos Antiques for about 60 years, then Jerry's Junque, Paradise Mountain Cafe, Curtin Call, Martini Hut, and Liberty Bistro. Clara and John Vos built it in 1933. They also ran the service station next door. Clara Vos was the Woodland Park town clerk from 1943 to 1946. (UPHS.)

The Donut Mill was built in 1901 as the Webb house. John Webb was the Colorado Midland stationmaster in Woodland Park. It has been the Donut Mill for the last 28 years. Many families from Woodland Park, as well as Colorado Springs, start their weekend treks in the mountains with a donut and coffee in hand. (UPHS.)

The Colorado Midland Railway reached Woodland Park in 1887, stopping at resort communities along the way. With travelers' ability to ride the train from Colorado Springs, tourism made its way to the mountains. Large, comfortable resort hotels were built, and hundreds of people came on excursions. The route was very scenic, and as the railway extended farther and farther into the mountains, more people came to witness the beauty. (UPHS.)

This is an old tuberculosis (TB) sanitarium with six-sided, tent-like cabins that were reportedly moved from Manitou Springs. These were later bridged with a newer building between them, and fieldstone was added to the base. These TB huts were more common in Colorado Springs and Manitou Springs in the early 1900s than in Woodland Park. This example is located between Rampart and Baldwin, about the 700 block. (UPHS.)

This is a family paddle boating on the lake in Memorial Park, located at the corner of Henrietta Street and Park Avenue. The lake is still sometimes used for ice skating in the winter and fishing contests each July Fourth. (UPHS.)

Local history buff Al Uebelhart moved to the Woodland Park area in 1977. He has gone for walks with his metal detector almost daily since then, looking for historic items. He has found most items not far from his home in Ridgewood. Here he looks at part of his collection of artifacts from the Manitou Park area. Like Uebelhart, tourists find many objects of historical interest every year along the old Ute Pass Trail, which was traveled by the Utes, trappers, homesteaders, railroaders, miners, and tourists. The traces of people from long ago are all around this area—arrowheads, cabins, mines, railroad ties, and other relics—as tangible reminders of the story of Westward Expansion. (UPHS.)

Five

GROWING AND HERDING ABOVE THE CLOUDS

Ranching and farming played an integral part in the early history of the Woodland Park area. The names of many pioneer homesteaders live on in the surviving ranches—or (more commonly) adorn the signs of today's subdivisions and streets. The larger ranches were located either north or west of Woodland Park, where there was abundant water and grass for grazing cattle and horses.

In the early days, there were about 3,000 head of cattle in the Manitou Park valley, with grass so tall it brushed the stirrups of the cowboys as they rode through it. As more settlers came to the valley in the late 1800s and early 1900s, many of them attempted to cultivate the open grasslands. The most common crops were potatoes, oats, winter wheat, rye, and head lettuce. The reasons for failure were many: the soil was infertile, the grazing season was too short, the rainfall was unpredictable, and economic conditions were depressed. Attempts at cultivation were abandoned in the 1930s.

North of town were the Clyde and Irene Denny ranch and the Tom and Edith Atwell ranch. The Dennys and Atwells used their tractors to dig postholes and stretch wire to help install the much-welcomed phone lines.

In the Manitou Park area, Henry T. Johns homesteaded 160 acres and leased 10,000 acres from Gen. William Palmer and his business associate, Dr. William Bell. Also homesteading were several families on Bald Mountain who ran cattle and raised hay and potatoes. The blizzard of 1913, one of the worst in Colorado history, buried parts of Bald Mountain under 20 feet of snow, leaving the residents homebound for two months. The Armentrout Ranch is still part of this beautiful but harsh landscape.

The Bob and Naomi Markus Ranch is one of the larger working ranches west of Woodland Park. Roger Holden's former Catamount Ranch is now the site of the private Catamount Institute and Teller County's Catamount Open Space. The adjoining Glenn Johnston ranch started as a dairy farm and continues to grow hay and raise cattle today.

This was the main house on the Spielman-Denny Ranch on Colorado State Highway 67 north of Woodland Park, around 1915. The Spielman family was among the earliest ranchers in the area, establishing their ranch around 1905. There they raised cattle and grew potatoes. In 1934, ranch ownership passed to Lewis Spielman's daughter Irene and her husband, Clyde Denny. (UPHS, Denny.)

Lewis Spielman loads his hay wagon after a productive summer with good rains on his ranch, around 1917. This was after days of following the horse-drawn sickle mower and rake. It was hot, dirty, lung-clogging work. The hay was later handfed into the baler. (UPHS, Denny.)

This is a harvesting scene in 1919 on what later became the Spielman-Denny Ranch. In the early years, the Spielman family harvested a great deal of hay, which grew abundantly in the high altitude and which the Spielmans needed in order to feed the large herd of cattle and horses. (UPHS, Denny.)

This picture shows a horse-drawn team hard at work during hay-threshing time in 1914 on the Spielman-Denny Ranch. People worked from sunup to sundown to bring in the hay. There was a very short growing season at such a high altitude, and snow could fall at any time during the haying season. (UPHS, Denny.)

Haystacks are shown on the Spielman-Denny Ranch in this 1914 photograph. Hay grew well in the Woodland Park area in those days, making it great cattle country. In an article in the *Colorado Springs Farm News* in 1932, Lewis Spielman talked about the success of cattle ranching in this part of the state and how huge herds of "little long-horned cows" were driven both to and from Texas. (UPHS, Denny.)

This 1897 grain drill was used on the Spielman-Denny Ranch north of Woodland Park. It was drawn by horses, with one person handling the drill and one person handling the horses. Using a drill allowed for consistent sowing of the seeds over large areas. Sometimes these drills were homemade. (UPHS, Denny.)

This is a picture at branding time with, from left to right, J. C. Locke, Ned Turner, L. J. Spielman, and an unidentified child in 1916 on their ranch just north Woodland Park. Branding was the culmination of rounding up the cattle, quite a job in itself, as it was mostly open range. Once the herd was rounded up, it was time for cutting out the calves to brand. This was quite a task in those days and still is today. (UPHS, Denny.)

This is a potato sorter at the Spielman-Denny Ranch north of Woodland Park. Ranchers in the area supplemented their income with potatoes, which grew very well in the area. Sorting potatoes in the early days was done by hand. Odd-sized potatoes were given to the cows. When the weather was cold and the potatoes were hard, the old timers said the cows would step on the potatoes and then eat them. (UPHS, Denny.)

This is a potato planter at the Spielman-Denny Ranch north of Woodland Park. Potatoes were a good cash crop for a long time, as local potato-growers had a ready market in Cripple Creek's miners during the early 1900s. Lewis Spielman described how they loaded up 100-pound bags of potatoes and hauled them by horse-drawn wagons. As mining declined, growing potatoes ceased to be profitable. (UPHS, Denny.)

This is a potato planter at the Spielman-Denny Ranch north of Woodland Park. Lewis Spielman said, "We'd get our seed potatoes and plow up the ground with a sulky plow pulled by three horses. Had an old homemade potato planter that we'd pull with a team. One fellow drive; one fellow sit up there and flip the potatoes back to go down the hole." (UPHS, Denny.)

This is an acreage marker on a grain drill at the Spielman-Denny Ranch north of Woodland Park. This was used to distribute the seed grain in a uniform manner in those early days of farming. The crops grown in those days included oats and barley, which grew well in the high altitude. (UPHS, Denny.)

Horse-drawn potato diggers like this one were a great improvement over the earlier method of harvesting potatoes by hand with a potato fork. Locally, potatoes were an important source of income in the area from around 1900 to the 1930s. A lot of the locally raised potatoes were raised for seed stock. (UPHS, Denny.)

This is an outhouse on the Spielman-Denny Ranch north of Woodland Park. The roof shingles make this a very nice outhouse for the times. These were hardy folks, the early settlers, wading through snow in the winter and dodging insects in the summer. A trip to the outhouse in the middle of the night could be quite an adventure. (UPHS, Denny.)

This is the interior of an outhouse on the Spielman-Denny Ranch north of Woodland Park. A two-holer was pretty luxurious in those days. Note the high and low seats, just right for adults and children. This was pretty convenient compared to those living in mining camps. Higher up in the mountains, two-story outhouses were used, as the snow was very deep there in the winter. (UPHS, Denny.)

This potato cellar was built around 1903 on the Spielman-Denny Ranch north of Woodland Park. The cellar was lined with rock and lime mortar, with pitch timbers to hold the roof and sawdust under the roof for insulation. Potatoes were kept over the winter in these cellars, which maintained a consistent temperature year round. (UPHS, Denny.)

This is Irene Denny on the Spielman-Denny Ranch north of Woodland Park, Colorado, in 1976. Irene still enjoyed using a wood-burning cook stove. Clyde raised 1,200 to 1,400 Hereford cattle. They hauled the cattle by truck to the Mary Ellen Ranch, which is now Fort Carson. They got 18¢ a pound there, which was more money than the Denver market paid. They retired from raising cattle in 1972. (UPHS, Denny.)

This is the Gayler KIE Ranch on Bald Mountain, east of Woodland Park on Rampart Range in 1938. G. G. Gayler homesteaded on the Rampart Range in 1908. They raised hay, potatoes, and cattle. Potatoes were their main source of income, as potatoes grew profusely up there. They owned both sides of the road. They had two ranches on Bald Mountain. The Gaylers ran a dude ranch business in the early 1920s until 1949, when G. G. Gayler retired. (UPHS, Gayler.)

Kie Gayler, the brother of G. G. Gayler, is on the plow. In 1906, G. G. Gaylor homesteaded land on Bald Mountain. The Gaylors raised cattle and later started a dude ranch in the 1920s. They also had about 60 horses at their Elkhorn Stables. At one point, G. G. Gaylor's son, Les Gayler, worked on a turkey farm in Crystola Canyon. (UPHS, Gayler.)

This is a picture of branding time at the Bell Ranch. Dr. William Bell was an early settler in the Woodland Park area, north on what is now Colorado State Highway 67. In 1872, this area was named Manitou Park by Dr. Bell. He eventually had 10,600 acres, of which some was used to raise cattle and some became the site of the Manitou Park Hotel, which was built in 1873. Dr. Bell supplied the hotel with his own beef. (UPHS Worden.)

The Lynch Ranch, located on South 40 road, was originally the Summit House and Stagecoach barn, a stopover in the late 1880s. The Colorado Midland Railway grade ran through the ranch. This is the original stagecoach barn. Travel in those days was on a rough dirt road and quite an adventure, especially in the winter. (UPHS.)

This photograph of the Lynch Ranch shows the house, stagecoach barn, and other outbuildings. The ranch was located in a very scenic but remote area. It was one of the earliest ranches in the area, founded during an eventful time not long after the Ute Indians were removed from the area, when the town later known as Woodland Park was beginning to develop. (UPHS.)

This 1989 photograph shows the Friendfield Turkey Ranch in Crystola. Friendfield had 12,000 turkeys and was said to be owned by famed author Laura Gilpin and Elizabeth Forster. They lived there in the 1940s. Laura Gilpin and Elizabeth deeded the Woodland Park Cemetery to the Town of Woodland Park. Laura Gilpin wrote *The Enduring Navajo* and *Enduring Grace*, her autobiography. (UPHS.)

This is a photograph of the icehouse on the Thunderhead Ranch. The ranch eventually consisted of 640 acres. The ranch extended from the Rampart Range to what is now Colorado State Highway 67. The Thunderhead Inn in Woodland Park is located where the original ranch house stood. The ranch raised cattle and caught wild horses in South Park, which it would train to use during hay season. (UPHS.)

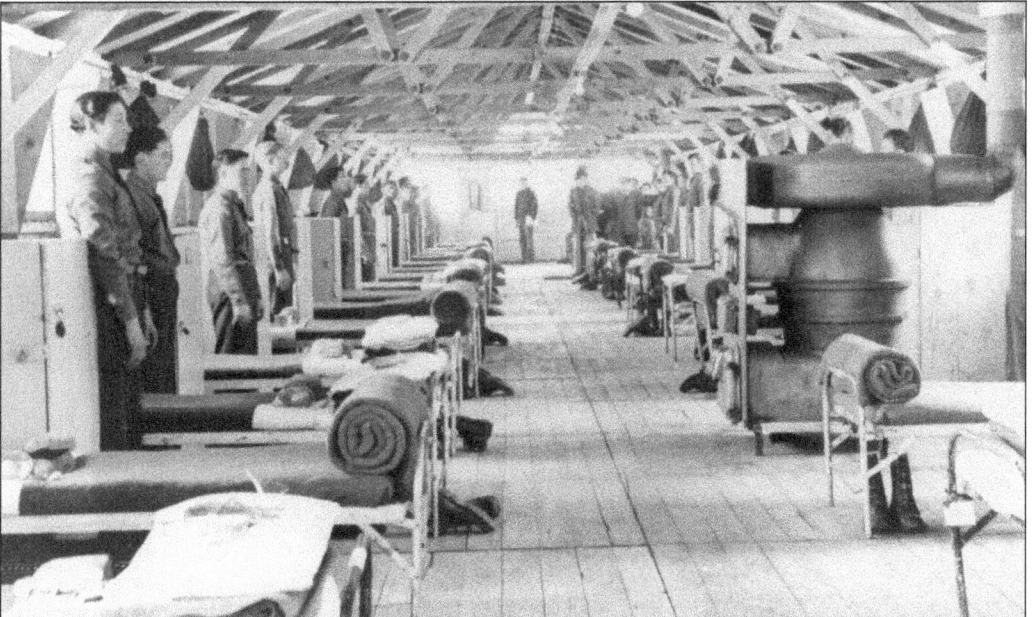

This is a picture from a barracks inspection at the Civilian Conservation Corps (CCC) camp at Painted Rocks, near Woodland Park in 1939. The CCC planted hundreds of trees and worked on roads and other improvements in the area. They were young men between the ages of 18 and 28 who came from families having financial difficulties during the Depression. (UPHS, George and Velma Worden.)

This is a panoramic view of the CCC camp. The men lived outdoors in camps and worked on conservation projects for Federal land management agencies. They built the Rampart Range Road in the Pike National Forest in partnership with the USDA Forest Service. They also planted acres of trees in what is now Meadowood Park. (UPHS, George and Velma Worden.)

This telephone pole in Manitou Park was left over from when phone lines were first strung to poles and trees so that the ranchers north of Woodland Park could get phone service. Edith Atwell and the grange members were given a "free use" permit across U.S. National Forest Service lands, but they had to provide their own insulators and wire. The Manitou Park Telephone Company was later incorporated as a non-profit. (UPHS.)

Six

DANCING, GAMBLING, AND HORSING AROUND

Area ranches proved to be the perfect venues for more than just ranching. They became the centers of Woodland Park's social life on many a weekend, with square dances and other types of dances sometimes lasting all night. Families brought their children, put them all to bed in one room, and then danced the night away. One night—this was before antifreeze was invented—it was 30 degrees below zero when a dance ended, and the guests had to pour hot coffee in their car radiators so they could drive home. Dances were also held at the Odd Fellows Hall, the local saloon, the school, and in the outdoor pavilion during the summer.

Gambling became a major pastime for miners and others in the 1890s and continued into the 1930s. Though one of the first ordinances of the newly formed town of Woodland Park in 1891 prohibited gambling, apparently the ordinance was not strictly enforced. Woodland Park had a reputation in the surrounding communities as a place to come for a good time.

The bars in Woodland Park became popular gambling places. Slot machines stood along the walls of both the Ute Bar and the Wrangler's Inn, while poker games were held continuously in the smoke-filled back room of John Harkins's bar. People even had slot machines in their homes—and legend has it that some still do. Soon enough, gambling casinos sprang up in town. The three most popular were the El Dorado (now a preschool), the Ouray Inn, and the Thunderhead. The Thunderhead was especially popular, offering gamblers free food and drinks, topless dancers from Las Vegas, liquor (provided from a still hidden in the woods), and numerous games, including roulette, blackjack, craps, slots, and poker. When federal agents cracked down on gambling in Woodland Park and its environs, gambling equipment found its way to hiding places in local barns as casino owners were tipped off to impending raids.

Finally, a number of resignations and appointments led up to the town elections in the spring of 1950. After the election, newly (and popularly) elected mayor Olin C. Little declined to take the oath of office, and Stacey P. Stuart was appointed to take his place. With the new mayor and a majority of the board of trustees opposing gambling, enforcement of the gaming laws became a top priority. As establishments reputed to have gaming tables and machines were raided, the slot machines and other gaming paraphernalia were loaded onto a truck and sent to Cripple Creek, the county seat. When the truck got to Cripple Creek, it was found to be empty. The story is that the driver stopped only once, in Divide, for coffee.

In 1916, the newly formed Woodland Park Rodeo Association held the first of many rodeos in the city. Men competed in traditional rodeo events, while women participated in horse races. The early rodeo association dissolved in the 1930s, but by the late 1930s, informal rodeos were being held once again. In 1948, organized rodeos returned and were held at a new location in the center of town. Fifty contestants participated in the first rodeo; within several decades, the number had risen to 250.

This is the way the Woodland Park lake and pavilion looked around 1910. The pavilion, which was built in 1890 and razed in 1949, hosted many community activities. (UPHS, Carroll.)

This pavilion, shown here in the 1890s, was a popular picnic spot. It was located at the top of a hill north of the Crest Hotel. In the front row, third from the left, is rancher and farmer William Roberts, who homesteaded at Thunderhead. At the top of stairs is his brother, Elmer Roberts. In the front row in the middle are Otto Theodore of Crystola and Sophia Longwell. (UPHS, Roberts.)

COLORADO.

THE WOODLAND PARK AMUSEMENT COMPANY

CAPITAL STOCK, $2,500.   250 SHARES.

This is to Certify that *C. W. Bowman*

THE WOODLAND PARK AMUSEMENT COMPANY,

Woodland Park, Colorado,

$10.00 EACH

This photograph shows Stock Certificate No. 1 for 10 shares in the Woodland Park Amusement Company, issued to Charles W. Bowman. It was signed by J. C. Carroll, secretary, and C. W. Bowman, president, on June 20, 1901. The Woodland Park Amusement Company built a baseball diamond on the west side of town just south of the Woodland Hotel. This area is about where Foxworth-Galbraith is now. Because of the blue laws in Colorado Springs forbidding Sunday baseball games, Woodland Park became a favorite Sunday destination for fans and was known as "the baseball park with a view." Players and spectators would ride the special Colorado Midland train up to Woodland Park, offload at the railroad spur in front of the hotel, take in the game, sightsee, and ride the train back to Colorado Springs in the evening. This lasted several years until Colorado Springs dropped out of the Western Baseball League. (UPHS.)

Square dancing has been a favorite activity of Woodland Park residents throughout the city's history. In the 1940s and 1950s, the square dances held at the Midland Avenue school proved to be a popular community event for the PTA. Ray Hope, who lived in Colorado Springs, frequently made the trip up Ute Pass to call the square dances. Somewhat later on, they were called by Francis Ware. (UPHS.)

The El Dorado casino at 312 North West Street was one of the more popular gambling parlors that sprang up in Woodland Park. It was built in 1932 by Bert Bergstrom and managed by Harley Inman and Loren Chamberlin. Bill Woods' father built the large ornate craps table for the casino. Since the 1990s, the former casino has been home to the Preschool in the Pines, a childcare center. (UPHS.)

This is another view of the El Dorado gambling casino at 312 North West Street. Teller County had developed a notorious reputation for gambling and all that goes with it. Slot machines were installed in almost every business in the community, including grocery stores, drug stores, and gas stations. Clubs and the back rooms of other establishments offered high-stakes poker, roulette, and dice games. Rumor has it that gaming in north Teller County was controlled by locals and that the area south of the Midland Terminal tunnel (known locally as "Little Ike") on Highway 67 was controlled via Canyon City by "New Orleans types." Another tale claims that Bert Bergstrom asked a friend to leave his new truck in the parking lot with the keys in it. Bert used the truck to dispose of gambling equipment. The truck disappeared with the equipment in it, and Bert replaced the truck. Bert was a businessman, but if they ever needed a handshake loan, he was there for his friends. (UPHS.)

The Ouray Inn was built in the 1940s by H. H. Robinson for LeRoy and Mickey McManaman from Texas. Homer Cooley managed the operation. It was a great place for an evening of fun, but membership was required. It was licensed as a private club, and new members needed to come recommended by other members. The Ouray became the Brazenhead Restaurant, then the Pikes Peak Museum. It is now an office building. (UPHS.)

The house built 200 feet west of the Ouray Inn in 1948 was the casino and also rumored to be a bordello. A local legend suggests that there was a tunnel between the two buildings. Jan Pettit's *Courier* article of January 11, 1990, reported that crooked dice and gaming paraphernalia were found. The building became the Rampart Range Public Library in 1983 and is now back in private ownership. (UPHS.)

During its gambling casino days, the Thunderhead Inn featured the small, cage-like building at right front where drunks and troublemakers could be temporarily incarcerated. Known for its excellent restaurant, the inn was purchased by Bert Bergstrom in the 1940s. High-stakes poker games were reportedly held in a nearby cabin. Each night, guests at a prominent Colorado Springs hotel looking for action were brought by limousine to the Thunderhead. Roulette, blackjack, craps, and slot machines were all available in the main building. The poker cabin is now located on the Murphy property next to the Thunderhead. Leoma Kelly, part of the morning clean-up crew, said it was a wonderful place for dinner and an entertaining floor show. Later on, the Saddle Club had their Christmas dinners there. Somewhere north of town, gaming establishments made their own booze. (UPHS, McTighe.)

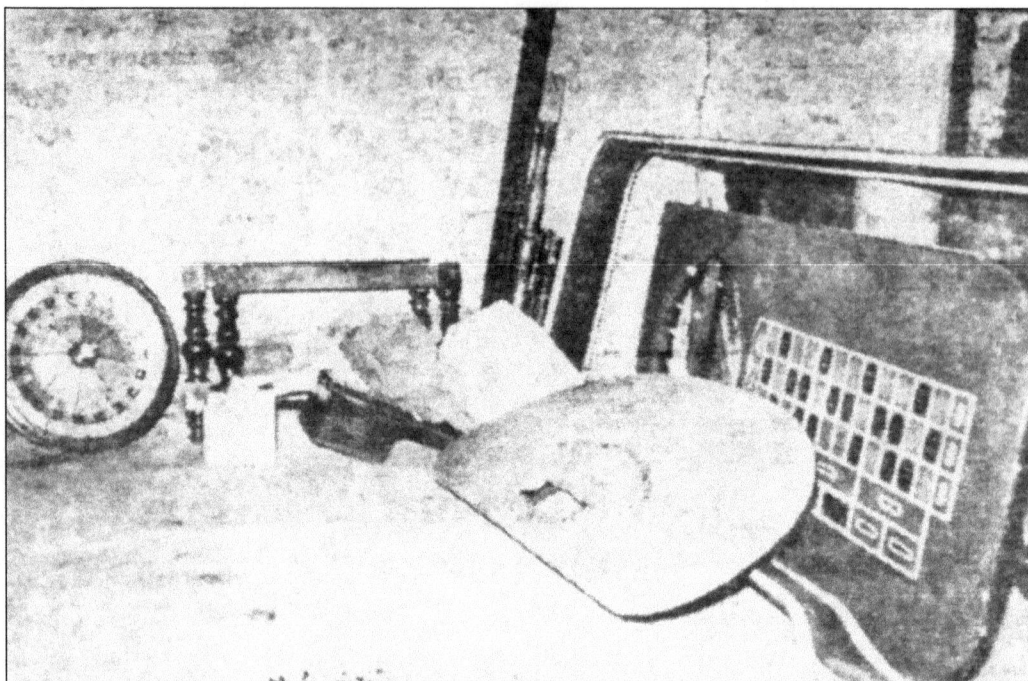

Gambling apparatuses confiscated from various places in Teller County are shown in this 1951 photograph that ran in the *Denver Post*. Crusading against Woodland Park gambling were pastor Robert E. Faulkner, mayor Stacy P. Stewart, and town marshal Curtis Weaver. Another *Denver Post* article reported that "slot machines and punch boards appear as commonplace as cash registers in five Teller County communities." (UPHS.)

The Ute Inn on Midland Avenue was bought by Bert Bergstrom in 1946 after he had spent some time in Cripple Creek. Bert was a colorful character, perhaps a little rough but liked by almost everyone. When asked about the bootlegging days, Bert said with a laugh, "men gargled loud and clear with bourbon. It was cheaper." The Ute was seized for back taxes; Bert paid and the Ute was reopened. (UPHS.)

This slot machine was reportedly given to Albert Putt by Bert Bergstrom. (UPHS.)

This photograph is of the Crystola Inn. Gabriel Brock was a boxer at Western State College and a Navy pilot in World War II. The original inn burned on December 7, 1941, and was rebuilt shortly thereafter. Brock and Inmann were owners in the late 1940s, and Brock became full owner in 1950. During that time, the Crystola hosted gambling in a back room. (UPHS, Cox.)

This is the location of a Prohibition-era still in Manitou Park, just north of present-day Ridgewood. A pile of barrel staves serves as a reminder of moonshine days. Les Gayler said Teller County's main occupation during the Prohibition era was bootlegging. He remembered several places in Woodland Park where one could obtain whisky for a dollar a pint. (UPHS.)

Bert Bergstrom poses in front of his Ute Inn on Midland Avenue. He was born in Sweden and came to the United States at age 17. His first residence was in San Francisco. He built the El Dorado, owned the Thunderhead Inn for a time, maintained a ranch north of town, and lived in the house where the Crest Hotel used to be. He donated land for Our Lady of the Woods Catholic Church's parking lot, for the Saddle Club Rodeo Grounds, and for the Bergstrom Park rest area. Bert is believed to have purchased the Midland Terminal right-of-way in parts of town, and even outside of town, for a nominal amount and to have given it to the landowners on both sides. He was the Grand Marshal for the Ute Trail Stampede rodeo parade for over 25 years. Bert also played Santa Claus to Teller County youngsters every Christmas for years. (UPHS, Ellett.)

This was Cal Elder's office. It is now the Carroll Den in History Park and houses the Colorado Midland Railway display. Elder sold insurance, served on the Teller County Board of County Commission and the city planning commission, and is credited with coining the phrase "City Above the Clouds." The name Carroll Den stems from the cabin's association with card games, held there when it belonged to the Carroll family. (UPHS, Elder.)

This is the grandstand at the old rodeo grounds across South Street from what is now city hall in the 1920s. Local residents participated in these rodeos. They were held on the Fourth of July, and only men competed in most events, though women did race horses. Dorothy Locke was a top competitor. Parades began in 1923. By the 1930s, rodeos moved east of town on land owned by Crowley. (UPHS, H. H. Robinson.)

Smith is riding on Aspen Glow in the bronco-riding event at the 1923 rodeo in Woodland Park. The early rodeos had no fences, only cars parked in a circle around the grounds. There was no separation between the livestock and the crowd. In this photograph, the contestants and spectators seem to be very dressed up for the occasion. (UPHS, Gayler.)

This is a photograph of a bronco rider in the 1922 rodeo. Since the contestants were all local men, everyone knew them, and they rooted for their favorites. There was a special three-day Wild West Show that year with a ball game at 10:00 a.m., followed by the rodeo events. There was also dancing day and night to the music of the Olinger's Highlanders 45-piece band. (UPHS, Gayler.)

This is Ralph Smith bull riding in the 1922 rodeo. These rodeos started in 1916 when ranchers and farmers decided rodeos would be fun, according to Irene Denny. Her uncle George Spielman and father, L. T. Spielman, were part of that group. L. T. Spielman was the president of the original rodeo association, and his brother was a board member. The event was called the Woodland Park rodeo. (UPHS, Gayler.)

Bud Hooling is bull riding in this photograph. Bull riding was indeed a rough and dangerous activity and often had a spectacular ending. According to many locals, these bulls were the meanest in the region. (UPHS, Gayler.)

This photograph shows a contestant who seems to be staying on this bull (for now). These bulls could weigh up to 1200 pounds, and staying on one took a lot of grit and muscle. Some of the World Rodeo Champions of the 1920s were bronco rider Yakima Canutt, steer wrestler Strangler Lewis, and steer/bull dogger Frank McCarroll. (UPHS, Gayler.)

Leonard Stroud is pictured bull riding at the Woodland Park rodeo in 1923. Another development was the establishment of parades. The first ones were around the arena. The arena stood where the city hall and the fire station now stand. Irene Denny remembered riding around the arena with a boyfriend and taking the prize for being the best on horseback one year. (UPHS, Gayler.)

This is a picture of Dewey Ronning, a contestant in the bronco-riding event at the Woodland Park Wild West Show. The photograph shows a large crowd close to the action. Back in 1921, the Wild West Show was granted a 20-year contract by the town of Woodland Park to use land in the town for the show. The land lay between West and Center, from Lake Street to Henrietta Street. (UPHS, Gayler.)

This photograph shows a man steer wrestling in a remarkable outfit. His shoes and hat are not the typical image of a cowboy that we know from Western movies. Steer wrestling was not new to cowboys, being a part of their ongoing job on the ranches. These rodeos were first held on the Fourth of July, then on Colorado Day. Money from spectator tickets went to local cowboys. (UPHS, Gayler.)

This man is steer riding at the rodeo in 1923. He is wearing a white shirt and tie. Also visible in this photograph are two pick-up riders anxiously waiting to assist this cowboy. The cowboy appears to be doing a good job staying on his steer. During these rodeos, unusual things sometimes happened. During one rodeo, a Brahma bull jumped a fence, scaring the spectators. (UPHS, Gayler.)

This is Woodland Park's rodeo. This photograph illustrates how the rodeos were conducted. Note the cars, which formed the rodeo ground around the ball field located in the center of town. Note the pavilion in the background, north of the lake. Rampart Range is on the horizon. (UPHS, Gayler.)

Fred Joiner was the overall winner in the 1923 rodeo. By the mid-1930s, rodeos were discontinued. The town government had options on many lots around the lake in 1938, but it wanted the five that the rodeo company owned. The town negotiated with L. J. Spielman and then John Carroll for six years until 1944, when they finally reached an agreement, and the company sold the lots to the town. (UPHS, Gayler.)

This photograph shows the Woodland Park Rodeo in 1948, when it was held north of town at the Paint Pony Ranch. The rodeos of the 1930s were a memory when the rodeo company decided to enter a log cabin float in the 1947 Colorado Springs Rodeo Parade. They took first prize, sold the float, and tried to decide what to do with the prize money. (UPHS, Barnes.)

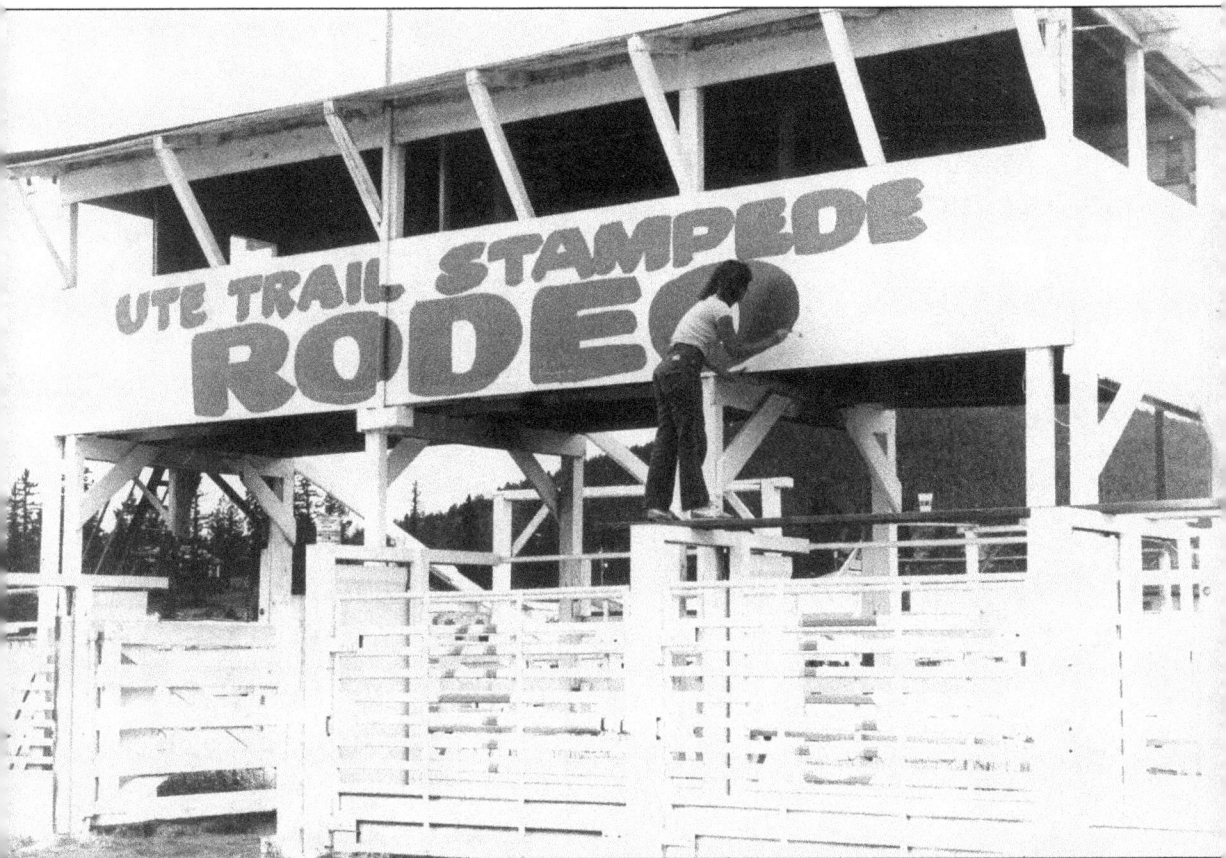

This photograph shows a lone sign painter adding finishing touches to the Ute Trail Stampede. They decided to use the prize money from the parade to start a Saddle Club and have a rodeo. Ira and Georgia Belle Hollingsworth, Ed and Anna Bean, Bob and Ethel White, George Klumph and his sister Catherine, Tom and Edith Atwell, and Walter Maximoff were the founders, with Ed Bean serving as chairman and Edith Atwell as secretary-treasurer. The Ute Trail Stampede rodeo was an annual event for more than 45 years, held on land donated by Bert Bergstrom. The popular rodeo attracted old-time cowboys, who camped out on the grounds for the weeklong event. The crowds were so large initially that the Saddle Club had to borrow portable bleachers from Fort Carson to accommodate the spectators. The club then built permanent seats, chutes, and an announcer's stand (UPHS, Carol Ellett.)

Annual
Wild West
Show

Contests Open to All

WOODLAND PARK, COLO.
August 1st, 2nd and 3rd, 1922

WOODLAND PARK
RODEO
July 18th, 1948

Sponsored by the Woodland Park Saddle Club

These rodeo programs highlight the Wild West Show held August 1-3, 1922. From 1916 to 1923, rodeos were staged by local ranchers, stock and all. After a lapse during the 1930s and early 1940s because the grounds and the show became too expensive, rodeos started up again in 1948 thanks to the Saddle Club. In 1948, the Ute Trail Stampede started but not without some growing pains. It rained for five days before the first rodeo opened, and when the first cowboy hit the ground, he slid halfway across the arena. In 1954, the club added the Little Britches Rodeo and later the Old-Timers Rodeo. (UPHS.)

This photograph of the 1947 rodeo parade shows riders from the Saddle Club. This was one of the last rodeos at the old rodeo grounds. M and H Garage, seen in the center of the photograph, was owned by Roy Monet and Frank Harbour. It was located east of where Buck's Saloon is today. At different times, Monet was a city trustee and Harbour was a mayor, school principal, and superintendent. (*Teller County Sentinel.*)

This photograph of the rodeo's grand parade, shot sometime before 1947, appears to have been taken just west of Memorial Park near the current city hall. Bald Mountain can be seen in the background. On the left is the pavilion; toward the center, the tower on the two-story school building is visible. (UPHS, Lynn Gayler.)

This photograph of Freia Hooper and her horse was taken at Paradise Ranch around 1965. She was the wrangler wife of Joe Hooper, the ranch foreman. Every spring, anticipating the arrival of the dudes, the Hoopers bought and traded hundreds of horses, hired 200 hands, including 25 wranglers, and handled the day-to-day chores for Frank Snell, who owned the ranch until about 1970. Cowboys and a few adventurous cowgirls brought their saddles and a bag full of clothes to hire on as wranglers. Freia I. Hooper said of the Paradise Ranch, "For the rodeo cowboy as well as wide-eyed Eastern greenhorn, first-rate Harry Vold rodeo stock promised chills, spills, and thrills every Sunday for the summer season. The guest's kiddies were not forgotten; they too lived in a fairy tale land for a week with their own ponies, their own coaches, and drivers." (*Roses and Locoweed*, UPHS; photograph bt Doris Breitenfeld.)

The first Ute Trail Stampede Rodeo Queen, Evelyn Workman (center), is shown with her aides, sisters Katie (left) and Jo Ann Brown. The election was held at the schoolhouse and used a penny vote system. Each vote cost a penny, so the election raised between $1000 and $1500 a year for the Saddle Club. The queen was crowned with a white Stetson hat, and her coronation ceremony was broadcast on KVOR radio. The Monty Montana trick riders were hired for the show that year. The queen for the second year was Katie Brown. The third year, Jo Ann Brown was elected queen, the festivities lasted two days, and the parade was 2 miles long. The queen and her aides were thrilled to be entertained at the Broadmoor Hotel by movie actor Gordon MacRae. That same year, a busload of about 40 convalescent soldiers from Camp Carson were invited to the rodeo. (*Colorado Springs Gazette Telegraph*, Friday, June 16, 1950.)

This photograph of the Paradise Ranch Rodeo south of U.S. Highway 24 shows the roof of the Paradise Lodge in the center background. The Paradise Ranch operated as a dude ranch and held a rodeo every weekend. They would roll out Frank Snell's collection of buggies and wagons with six- and eight-up teams for the grand entrance. (UPHS, Barnes.)

The Ute Trail Stampede Rodeo Parade, in July of 1956, passed by a food market operated by the Breitenfeld family. Since 1967, the store has been the site of the Cowhand Western wear store originally owned by Howard and Joan Stull. It is now owned by Marty McKenna, Merry Jo Larsen's daughter. Participating in the parade was the Teller Company Mounted Sheriff Posse. Lloyd Stoner Jr. was the flag bearer. (UPHS, Stoner.)

Two men pose with four recently killed deer in an "Our Game" Wellington photograph from the late 1800s. Whoever was counting only saw the four does hanging on the poles; a buck is also hanging on the tree and another on the vertical pole. This was back when hunters didn't have to draw for a single deer tag and be concerned with which season it was, or whether they were allowed to hunt with a bow, black powder, or a rifle. (UPHS, Wellington.)

Seen here from left to right, the members of this hunting party included John Carroll, Hunter Carroll, Allen Thompson, Ike Collins, Bill Cobb, George Sadler, Allie Gudger, Millare Campbell, and A. H. Thomson. The photograph was taken during the 1930s; hunting and fishing continue to be popular today in the area surrounding Woodland Park. (UPHS, Abbott.)

In this c. 1970 photograph, hikers follow the tracks of the No-Name Railroad just west of Ridgewood, a short distance east of Trout Creek. The lumbering railroad ran about 8 miles from end to end. This photograph was taken around 1970. (UPHS, Ubelhart.)

Sledding has always been a popular pastime, especially for the younger set. In earlier times, skis were strictly utilitarian, used for travel and getting chores done in the wintertime. People would take boards, soak them, and steam them to turn the ends. From 1963 to 1973, Harlan Nimrod ran a ski area at what is now Holiday Hills south of Edlowe. The Nimrods started it for their own children but opened it to the public. (UPHS.)

This photograph shows a motorcycle ice race at Rainbow Falls. At one time, the area shown here was part of Dr. Bell's Manitou Park Hotel and Ranch. For the last 35 or so years, in late fall after the lakes freeze, the enthusiasts tune up their motorcycles (and now ATVs) to go racing. (UPHS.)

Ice skating at Memorial Park was especially popular in the 1940s and 1950s. Chet Koons, a local electrician, installed lights for the skaters in the 1950s. Another location for outdoor activities in those days was the Catamount Ranch, where snow tubing and tobogganing were popular. Skating continues today at additional locations around the area, including Meadowood Sports Complex, which boasts an ice hockey rink. (UPHS.)

To celebrate the nation's bicentennial and Colorado's centennial, the city dedicated a time capsule that was sealed in a sundial cylinder and partially buried on the front lawn of Woodland Park City Hall. Shown at the ceremony are, from left to right, Councilman Bruce Kristoff, centennial chairman Bob Bergman, capsule chairman Courtney Willis, and city manager Glenn Bolsen. (*Teller County Sentinel,* August 5, 1976.)

This photograph shows the Olympic torch as it passed through Woodland Park at 10 a.m. on February 1, 2002, in advance of the Salt Lake City Winter Olympics. Well-wishers were out in force to cheer the local runners. The torch continued on through Teller County to Divide, where children from Summit Elementary came out from school to watch. (UPHS.)

This is the Hathaway home on South Forty Road, so named because of its connection with the former southern portion of U.S. Highway 40. The home features many of Paul Hathaway's metal sculptures, which also adorn many other local homes and businesses. His Western Frontier furniture brand was popular as far away as London; he once shipped an entire bedroom suite to the governor of Illinois. (UPHS.)

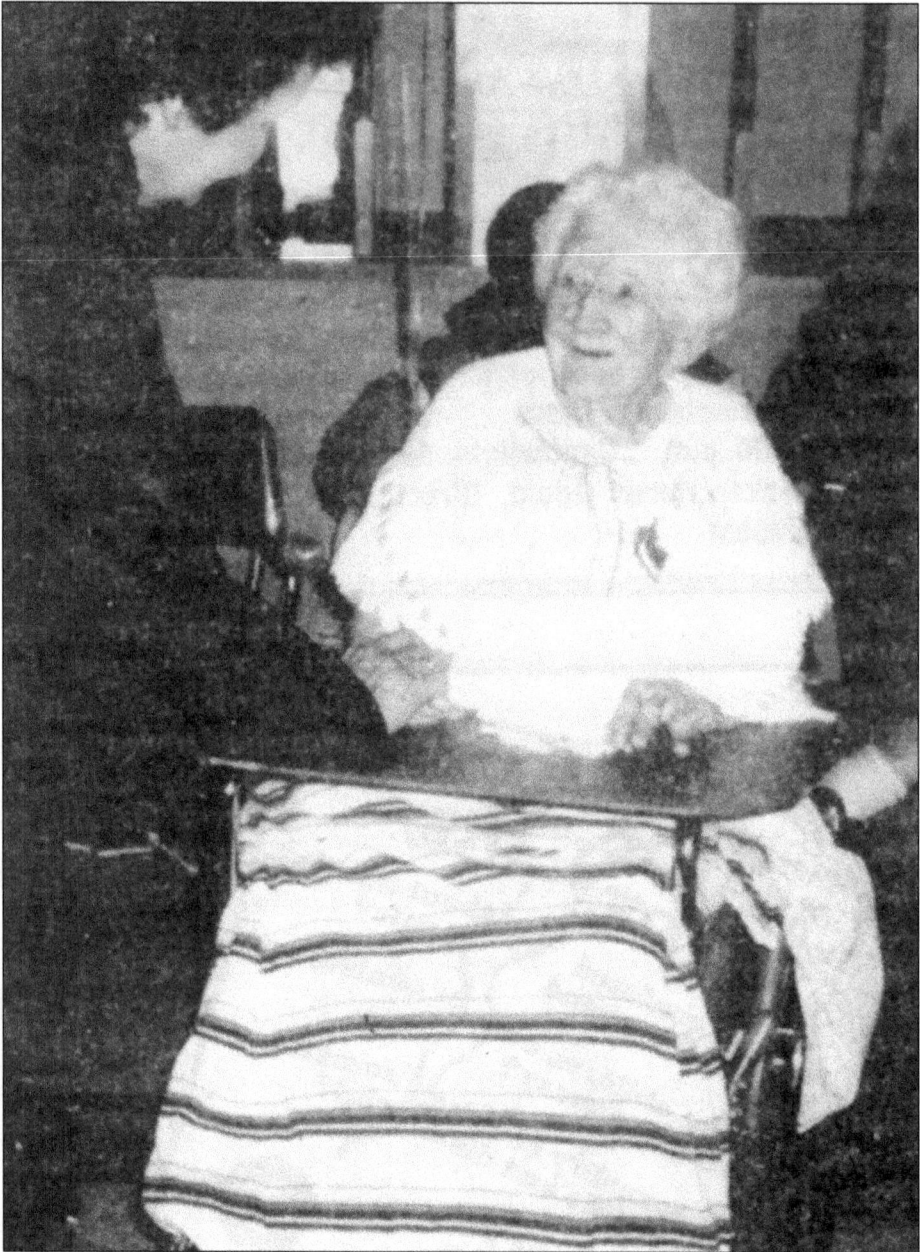

This photograph shows Clara Vos celebrating her 100th birthday on February 17, 1990. Of Dutch descent, Clara was born in Holland, Michigan. She was older than the town of Woodland Park, which incorporated January 26, 1891. She had been a resident of Woodland Park for almost 60 years. She and her husband, John, bought land in Woodland Park on Midland Avenue. The businesses they created there included rental cabins, a filling station, and Vos Antiques. They were longtime contributors to the fabric of the community. Clara was the city clerk for several years, and John was one of the first building inspectors. She had received the oldest-member pin of the Extension Homemakers Club nine years before. The Homemakers Club was established in 1936 and had a motto of "For Home, Health, and Social Improvement." Clara ran in seven of the Pikes Peak foot races. (Ute Pass Courier February 1990.)

UTE PASS HISTORICAL SOCIETY

The Ute Pass Historical Society was incorporated in 1976 as a non-profit corporation to collect, preserve, and interpret regional historical material, and to stimulate interest in the history of the Ute Pass area by collecting historical artifacts and providing programs of historical relevance. The first displays of its collection were in a rustic cabin in Green Mountain Falls. The displays were moved and expanded in a new home in Cascade. The collection's next move was to the Brazenhead in Woodland Park, but this move was short-lived. The Ute Pass Historical Society and the Pikes Peak Museum now reside in History Park in Woodland Park. The society's collections include manuscripts, oral interviews, and an extensive photograph collection including the historic Wellington photographs. With its collection of historical cabins and displays, the History Park provides a living display of the Ute Pass region's cultural heritage. It features Ute Indian artifacts and items from Ute Pass and the Pikes Peak area.

Each year the society sponsors a potato soup supper celebrating the area's agricultural and ranching heritage. On December 22, 1999, Representative Joel Hefley (R-CO) announced that the Ute Pass Historical Society's video *Pikes Peak Shadow*, detailing the 100-year history of Teller County, would represent Colorado's Fifth Congressional District in the national Local Legacies project of the Library of Congress's Bicentennial celebration to record the unique cultural traditions of America.

Visit us at
arcadiapublishing.com